THE OTHER JOE

Joseph P. Niland, Deacon
Annunciation Church
Paramus, NJ

ISBN: 1492937304
ISBN 13: 9781492937302

DEDICATION

This book is dedicated to my wonderful wife who I affectionately referred to as "Love Bubble" or by the name with which her friends knew
her, "Maureen." Also, to my sons Denis, Brian and John who sacrificed
so much to become the great people they are today.
And to Jesus Christ, without Him, I am nothing; and with Him I have
found nothing to be impossible.

A SPECIAL THANKS

Father Joseph Kwiatkowski of Annunciation Parish in Paramus, NJ was the moderator of a thirty-week program named, "JustFaith," in our Parish. Hence, I became "The Other Joe."

Initially, I participated just to be supportive of Father Joe. The group of 18 parishioners exhibited the great spirit of our Parish. As this program ended, we recognized each other as brother and sister and as a group united in love to help make this world a happier place. Hopefully, my book will not be a disappointment to them; they were the ones that encouraged me to write it.

Frieda Girolamo, my friend for 45 years was kind enough to edit the book for me. She spent countless hours correcting my grammar. Her infinite patience will always be remembered.

Our "JustFaith" Members are:

Rev. Joseph Kwiatkowski (Moderator)

Marlene Anthony	Susan Lindstrom
Santa Crisall	Elizabeth M. Marsh
Jim Dade	Marie McVeigh
Joan Dade	John J. McVeigh (R.I.P.)
Frieda Girolamo	Margaret McVey
Kristina Hayes	Margaret M. Moore
Barbara Hynes Hannon	Joe Niland (The Other Joe)
Tim Kupetz	Bud Nugent
Kevin Vogel	Marianne Windt

BIOGRAPHY OF JOSEPH NILAND

Author of "The Other Joe"

Born the son of Irish immigrants, I was raised in Washington Heights in New York City at a time when the country was at war. Both of my parents were touched by the Depression after coming to the United States and practiced the creed of signing nothing and saving every dollar. My dad worked as a mason for the Transit Authority and my self- educated mom, like most moms of that time, was a stay -at-home mother. We lived in a five-room apartment on the second floor of a six story building on 160th Street.

Having been weaned on Irish music, going to Gaelic Park every Sunday to see my dad hurl, and having my homework scrutinized by parents, who had no formal education, was not optional. Their values were reinforced by the nuns, religious brothers and priests that educated me. My mom told me that she cried when she came to this great country and saw the Statue of Liberty for the first time because she didn't feel worthy to be here. My two brothers and I cherished these same sentiments.

When I reached my eighteenth birthday, I had no money for college and I couldn't get a job because I was of draft age. Therefore, after an abbreviated college career, I enlisted in the Marine Corps. After three years, I met the girl of my dreams and two years later we were married. Initially, we lived in the Bronx, but later moved to Paramus, New Jersey. We not only raised a great family but took into our home over three hundred children. Each child had a different story to tell. My wife and I had a deep faith in God and He gave us a life of adventure, love and challenge. In 1976, after the Second Vatican Council, I was ordained a Catholic Deacon. It was a thrill when my children handed my vestments to me and I received the Sacrament of Holy Orders at Sacred Heart Cathedral in Newark, New Jersey.

Forty-two of my years were spent at the Automobile Club of New York. During most of this time, I was a supervisor and teacher. I finished my career at the AAA Phone Center in Newburgh, NY. Ten years were spent commuting to Garden City, Long Island, NY. The Cross Bronx Expressway taught me patience and humility and it became a time of prayer.

My wife passed away in 2002. She had cancer. My three sons have homes in Paramus. We are all active in our community.

My book outlines the way we lived, shared our lives with others, and fought discrimination and injustices while at the same time enjoyed and continue to enjoy life to its fullest.

INDEX

CHAPTER	TITLE	PAGE
Chapter One	Growing up in Washington Heights	1
Chapter Two	Life as a Teenager	15
Chapter Three	A Few Good Men	29
Chapter Four	Love at First Sight	43
Chapter Five	Wedding Bells	55
Chapter Six	Our First House	67
Chapter Seven	The Automobile Club of New York	81
Chapter Eight	Our Home in Paramus	91
Chapter Nine	A Revolting Development	99
Chapter Ten	Doesn't Anyone Care?	107
Chapter Eleven	Ordination	117
Chapter Twelve	Phil and Paul	127
Chapter Thirteen	Trials, Tribulations and Accomplishments	133

Chapter Fourteen | A Trying Act of Mercy | 141

Chapter Fifteen | A Deacon at Work | 149

Chapter Sixteen | Amen | 165

Epilogue | 171

GROWING UP IN
WASHINGTON HEIGHTS

Mom and dad were devout believers in our Catholic faith. We lived in Washington Heights, a section south of the George Washington Bridge and north of Harlem. Our apartment was on the second floor of a six-story walk up. We had three bedrooms, a kitchen, bathroom and living room. The floors were covered in loud-colored linoleum. Motif hadn't been invented. My brother, Frank, shared a bedroom with me. I slept on the side of the wall and for some reason licked the lead- based paint during my sleeping hours. Our window looked down on the backyard. On occasion, beggars would sing or perform with musical instruments and Frank and I would wrap buttons in pieces of paper and throw it to them. Thinking we gave them money, they'd bow in thanksgiving, pick up the buttons and yell threatening comments at us. At times they'd use vulgarities, but they never made good on their threats. One time, we thought our mother was doing the wash but she caught us at our chicanery. She warned us that she'd tell our dad and we had to keep the window closed for a week. All the windows had guards to protect brats like us from falling into eternity.

When I was three years of age, the Japanese bombed Pearl Harbor. My memory of the event was telling everyone what I heard. Naturally, I had no idea where Pearl Harbor was but it changed my neighborhood drastically. The men went off to war. Every window in the neighborhood proudly displayed flags with stars proclaiming their husband or son was an enlisted man or officer. Many women, especially those without children, gained employment in the war effort and everyone had books of coupons, which they needed to get an allotment of basic essentials. Our family traded off coffee coupons for tea. There were even restrictions on gasoline, but who owned a car? Certainly, none of my neighbors!

My Uncle Paddy, who lived in Brooklyn, owned an old Ford with a running board and this was my transportation to Misericordia Hospital where my youngest brother, Frank, was born. Uncle Paddy wanted to swap his car for my brother but I turned him down in an eye blink. Paddy was my Godfather and took a special interest in me. He used to take me places with his family. I remember traveling on the cobblestone streets of the Lower West Side where the piers were located. One day I saw the Queen Mary, the Queen Elizabeth, the United States and the Normandie, which was lying on its side. It was my understanding that this ship, which was the pride of the seas, was in the United States when the Germans invaded France. We kept it here to convert it to a troop transport. All its luxurious fixtures were removed and welders accidentally set it on fire. The New York City Fire Department pumped so much water into it that it sank. Finally, it was stripped for metal for the war effort. The Government was desperate for any kind of metal. One of the popular ways of salvaging was bringing old-fashioned irons for entry to the movies. They were the kind you'd heat on the oven range and had no cord.

There were so many different nationalities and ethnic groups in our neighborhood, and yet my brothers and I never knew what prejudice was all about. Our country had just come out of a Depression and everyone seemed too busy eking out a living to realize that a neighbor wasn't an Irish immigrant like my parents. Besides, if you made fun of another person's race, creed or color, you received a sentence of flogging with my dad's razor strop. Looking back, I now realize that the strop fell off its mark but always hit an object that resounded loudly. Fear is certainly an effective teacher.

In those years, there were few Asians in the New York City area. When one was seen, the onlookers more often than not pointed at them and accused them of being Japanese. A Chinese laundry was located on Amsterdam Avenue between West 160th and West 159th Streets. The premises also served as their living quarters. These poor immigrants spoke little English. The Japanese persecuted their people and now they were the focal point of persecution, oppression and prejudice. I don't think their two kids went to school. Rocks were frequently thrown through their shop window.

I can remember feeling their anxiety in such a cruel world. Even the cops showed little interest in their problem. My mother pointed out to me how cruel people can be and asked me to pray for them.

In those years, my cousin, Helen, came to live with us. She was in her late teens and very good looking. She was also a bobby soxer and adored Frank Sinatra. There was a sailor named Frank who wanted to date her. His brother worked with my dad for the Transit Authority. She said she'd go out with him if he got each one of us a sailor hat. He did and he took her out to a movie and dinner. Meanwhile, we sported our hats until they were filthy. Finally, my mother collected them and gave them a good bleaching. She then hung them on our clothesline, which was a rope between two buildings. The next morning they were gone. My father put the word out but without any favorable results. Finally, my dad spotted a teenager with one of the hats. Frank's last name was stenciled on each of them. He threatened the delinquent and gave him an ultimatum. The hats mysteriously reappeared hours later.

Although most of the men were called to war, my father remained rated as 1A by the Selective Service. I was always afraid he'd be drafted and ran down to get the mail every day praying that he wouldn't be taken away from us. He avoided the draft by having three children and his job as a mason for the Transit Authority didn't hurt either. My dad always preached job security. He was one of Mike Quill's supporters and a real union man. Dad didn't believe in college. He'd preach, "Become a Cop!"

At one time, my dad got very sick. He had contracted spinal meningitis and was lying in bed semi-comatose and the light made him plead for darkness. In desperation, Doctor Farley, who had received a citation from President Franklin Roosevelt for his medical excellence, asked my mother to sign an authorization to try a new drug. She complied and within a few days, dad turned the corner. His health improved and he survived spinal meningitis, which was frequently fatal in those days. The name of the drug was penicillin.

During the war, my cousin Helen's sister, Bea, and her husband, Larry arrived one day unexpectedly with their young son Terry. Larry was a Nuclear Physicist and spoke in polysyllables. My dad hardly understood him. He felt there was something wrong with Larry. Their marriage was on the rocks and Larry had to go to White Sands, New Mexico on a secret government mission. No children were allowed. They asked my parents if they could care for the baby for approximately six months. My mom and dad took the baby and set up a crib in their bedroom. When things got hectic, my dad would ask my mom in his Galway brough, "What the hell is the United States Government doing sending Larry into the desert; they must be having him build a bomb." Many years later, we determined that Larry worked on the Manhattan Project (The A-Bomb), America's most closely guarded secret.

It was a sad day for me when Larry and Bea returned to take Terry home. It was like losing a brother. I cried for days.

As the war ended, there was dancing in the streets and block parties throughout the city. The GI Bill allowed veterans not only educational benefits but mortgages on houses and many families moved to the suburbs. However, it seems we were anchored in the Heights. It was a long six blocks to Saint Rose of Lima where Dominican Nuns taught my brothers and me. There were fifty-two neatly uniformed students to each classroom and no one suffered from Attention Deficit Disorder; as a matter of fact, I don't think that malady had been invented. We wore a blue suit, blue tie and a clean white shirt every day. On occasion, a Sheaffer washable blue glob of ink covered our shirt pockets because everyone's pen leaked at one time or another. Also, the inkwells on each desk would allow the ink to dribble between the well and the paper. After a dip, the ink would frequently get on your hands. Ballpoint pens were finally introduced but they leaked worse and their ink was permanent. They became taboo because of the expense of buying shirts. Furthermore, they were expensive and weren't perfected. The nuns were loving but ruled the roost. They wielded yardsticks and pointers. Even a stick of chalk could be used as a weapon. If they ever complained about your school performance to your parents, no excuse was acceptable; not even a death certificate. When your parents got the word, you were in serious trouble. Boys and girls shared the same classrooms. In the upper four grades, the boys were on one side of the room and the girls on the other.

On Sundays, we wore our one and only suit that was not a uniform. It was always new on Easter Sunday but as the year went on, the pants became shorter and showed wear because we'd play ball on the way home from church. One year, my mother bought me a suit with knickers. This was the worst suit in my life. Naturally, I had numerous pictures taken with our Kodak "Brownie" camera to document how much I despised those pants.

My brother, Frank, was a good student. He was my dad's favorite. He was referred to as, "The Old Man." My brother, Larry, got away with murder. He was my mom's favorite but a problem for the nuns. My mom had the gift of blarney and always helped him get out of trouble. Larry was a natural athlete and was extremely good looking. On the other hand, I had thick glasses and was always getting into devilment. I really didn't mind being the middle son. I was given plenty of love and I used to operate below the radar. I did very well in grammar school. Despite this, the nuns tried to talk my parents into sending me to a special school because of my poor eyesight. At one point, they put a patch over my good eye to strengthen the muscle in my bad eye. Boy, did I pray! I think I had the best marks in my class that year but the saving grace, I'm sure, was that my parents didn't have the money for special schools. The nuns and I got along pretty well, but I always had to sit in the front of the room because they treated me as though I was blind. Actually, I had decent vision with my glasses.

Art was my favorite subject. I can recall when we had the classroom assignment of drawing windmills. Wow! I thought I had a masterpiece. This was the best I had ever done. Then I looked at the other kids' work and much to my surprise, my windmill was one inch smaller. The art teacher, Mrs. O'Rourke, went on a rampage and chased me with a yardstick. I ran into the closet. She demanded that I come out but I figured I'd only get beaten, so I stayed in the closet until the bell sounded; as my father would say in his thick Irish brogue, "Bad luck to her!" He wouldn't have stood for any teacher hitting me unless she was a nun. It's amazing to think that there was no tuition. Of course, there were always fundraisers and participating in them was mandatory.

When I got out of school, I used to team up with my great boyhood buddy, Vinny. We used to do things that were unacceptable in the adult world. We knew every shortcut in the Heights and loved going to Riverside Drive. We'd play handball and work out on the exercise bars. When asked where we were, the stock answer was, "Out."

Once, we broke the lock to an underground street underneath the Henry Hudson Parkway at West 157th Street. When the door opened, we saw the dark street that ran for blocks under the road's surface. Naturally, we went inside and embarked on an exploration mission. We were playing tag. Vinny was, "it," so I hid behind a steel pillar. There was something under my feet. When I looked closer, I realized it was a dead body. Shivers went up and down my spine. It was the first dead body I had ever seen that wasn't in a casket at Kelly's Funeral Parlor. The body was badly decomposed and resembled skeletal remains dressed in clothes resembling rags. Goose bumps rose immediately, and a chill ran through every cell of my body. Vinny and I ran about eight blocks to the 30th Precinct to report our findings. When we walked in, the Sergeant behind the desk was talking to several people. We were anxious to give him the news but he said, "Shut up and wait your turn." We were about eight or nine at the time. Therefore, we waited our turn to speak. After spending about twenty minutes taking care of other people's business, he said to us that he was out of PAL Baseball tickets; but we said we were there to report a murder. He asked, "Why didn't you tell me right away?" and sarcastically asked, "Who did you kill?" We then told him about our experience. He instructed two officers to drive us to the location where they found a badly decomposed body of a man, probably a poor homeless individual. Later, we got a ride home in the patrol car. The cops put on the siren for part of the trip and this really made our day.

There were plenty of homeless people and drifters in those days. Whenever one would knock on our door for a handout, my mother would have them sit down outside our door on a step and fix a meal for them. She would put the plate on a chrome tray. She'd then put a linen napkin on it and never left out a dessert. She then insisted that I sit and talk to the man. She felt no one should be left alone when they are eating. She said that a man is only poor if he's alone. Mom had a real sense of community. She loved everyone and was always doing something to help a neighbor.

Whenever my buddy, Vinny, and I could, we were drawn to the Hudson River. Once, I went out on a raft in the cold of winter. I was wearing a navy blue turtleneck sweater that my mother knitted. The raft certainly wasn't seaworthy. The Hudson River Dayliner went by creating waves and cast me into the drink. Fortunately, I discovered I could swim and managed to get to shore. I was sopping wet. We built a fire and I put my sweater near it. When I was somewhat dry, I went to put on the sweater. There was a white ash on the sleeve and when I wiped it off, a three-inch hole appeared. I told my mom that I put it near a fire to get warm. I'd never tell her that I was in the river. If I did, I wouldn't have seen water until I was twenty-one. However, I suspected that she might have known. That sweater didn't smell so great.

Those days were different. Vinny and I used to buy loosies, three cigarettes for a nickel. We even got a wooden match to light the cigarettes. We used to earn money when the rich people would drive their cars and park them on our block when they were going to the Polo Grounds. We'd just say, "Want us to watch your car for a quarter?" They would give us the quarter because they figured we'd damage their vehicle if they didn't.

No one owned a television set. At night, families would gather around the family radio and listen to the news. Gabriel Heater had the "in" news program and would begin each show with "There's bad news tonight." My father would always react the same way: "Oh dear God!" Kids would listen to "The Lone Ranger," and Nedick's Orange Drink had a sports show, which brought you up to date on the baseball scores for the Yankees, Giants and Dodgers. The sound effects stunk but that was all that was on for sports junkies. Then we'd join the adults and listen to "Fibber Magee and Molly" and "Baby Snooks." There was no Super Bowl and there were three baseball teams in New York. The biggest rivalries were the Dodgers and Giants. It cost twenty-five cents for a bleacher ticket at the Polo Grounds. If you didn't have a quarter, you could climb the wall and get in for nothing.

Still, our greatest love was the Hudson River. One day, army rafts that we suspected came from West Point floated down the river. There must have been ten of them. Each one was approximately four foot by ten. We picked the one that was in the best shape. It had a floor that was made of latticed wood. We put it under the pier at West 157th street. We even sawed a hole in the dilapidated pier and installed a crude ladder so we could get onto the raft without anyone knowing about it. We also put a trap door over the ladder and found wood that served as oars. About two weeks later, the weather was perfect so we embarked on our excursion to New Jersey. However, the tide pulled us into New York Harbor. We couldn't get back and we jokingly laughed because we were headed for Europe. Our mood changed quickly when the huge freighters caught our attention. We figured we had it. Fear replaced the laughter but then we saw what appeared to be a Navy vessel. Sure enough, it was the Coast Guard. They took us on board with our raft in tow, chewed us out and brought us back to the piers. They took our name and address and said they'd tell our parents. They were upset when we asked for our raft back. Naturally, we gave them misinformation and aliases. We never heard another thing about our episode.

The next day, we went back to the river. When we got there we noticed something floating on the water. We had a stick and attempted to reach out and pull it in. Sure enough, it was the body of a person. We couldn't tell if it was a man or a woman. The stick we had went right through the torso. It was so soft. It must have been in the water for weeks. Back again we went to the 30th Precinct. This time the big Irish Sergeant recognized us and called out to his buddies. "The kid's back!"

They all laughed but shuttered when we told them we found another body.

All together, we found five bodies. There were the two I already mentioned, the baby in the garbage can, and one more in the river. Oh yes, I don't know if you count the one that jumped off the George Washington Bridge onto land. There were other witnesses but we also reported it to the big Irish Sergeant. Every time I'd enter that police precinct, there would be a shout, "The kid's back!" However, he used to save us PAL (Police Athletic League) tickets for the Yankee games; which were my favorite. Vinny hated baseball and didn't care if he ever saw a game.

One time we were at the Hudson when it was frozen over at the shoreline. We figured we'd go out on the ice. It then became a challenge and we competed with each other to see who could go out the farthest. We had gone out about fifty yards when there was a cracking noise. It sounded like lightening! We started floating on little chunks of ice. We jumped from one cake to another and made it to shore without even getting wet. We then laughed and proceeded to walk along the path towards the exercise bars. Then we heard sirens and saw the police and fire engines following us. We then realized that some of the rich women who were looking out their windows on Riverside Drive saw us and called the cops. We started pointing the other way indicating that there were two boys that were on the ice and ran. They didn't believe us. The fire trucks left, but the cops blasted us. We still denied we were involved. They took our names and told us they'd tell our parents. Again, we gave them aliases and never heard another thing about it.

There was never a dull moment near the Hudson. It was a good thing my parents never knew the things we did.

My buddy, Johnny Coffey, and I had a project in school. We were in the same class. Johnny struggled through school and his mom and dad were always on his case. He used to pal around with Vinny and me as much as he could; but his sister had a grapevine that was flawless, and he always got into trouble.

We had a project concerning the American Indian. We were in luck because the Museum of the American Indian was a few blocks away. We went there and we were enthralled over the artifacts that appeared in the showcases. We spent countless hours writing notes and we were convinced that we'd get a hundred. This project was right up our alley. When we noticed it got dark, we figured we'd be on our way. When we tried to get out of the building we saw that it was locked up tight. Now it got dark and spooky. We wanted to break the glass but the building had a sacred aura about it and we figured we'd be thrown in jail if we did any damage, so we slept in the museum or at least tried. As soon as the doors were unlocked in the morning, we ran home. Our pace quickened because on the way, neighborhood kids laughed and yelled, "You're going to get your asses kicked." My parents would have killed me but I put on the tears and told them and what happened, I said I was petrified and they hugged and forgave me. Johnny and I couldn't see each other for a month. That was a pretty lenient sentence.

After Johnny and I finished our sentence, we celebrated by going to High Bridge Swimming Pool. When we got there, we brought along some loosies and lit up in a no smoking area. This caught the eye of a cop and he caught us red handed. He threw us in an equipment closet and said we'd spend the rest of the day in the sweltering heat. Johnny and I came up with a flawless plan. After a half hour or so, I hollered, "My friend isn't breathing!" The cop went into the panic mode. As he opened the door, we were history. He screamed, "I'll get you two!" but he never did.

My father had a cigarette lighter that only he could touch. This made it as appealing as the apple in the Garden of Eden. On my eighth birthday,

I took it out of his drawer and into the bathroom. I lit one piece of toilet paper after another.

The longer the piece of paper, the more thrilling the experience; until the plastic curtains caught fire and I got desperate. My efforts to douse the flames were in vain. Because the situation was hopeless; I retreated to the living room and proceeded to listen to the family radio with my mother. She took a breath and detected a hint of smoke. She asked, "Joseph, do you smell fire?" Naturally, I said "No." Certainly, I wasn't about to throw myself under the bus. My answer didn't satisfy her. She got up and proceeded down the long hallway that led to the kitchen, a bedroom and the inferno in the bathroom. She yelled, "Oh my God!" and fought the blaze like a professional firefighter. When she was sure every flame was extinguished, she came back to the living room, sat down and gave a sigh of relief. After she got her composure, she inquired if I had any idea how the fire could have started. I presented the possibility that it could have been the kids who lived upstairs in our six-story building. Frequently, I observed them throwing matches out the window and one of them must have blown in the window. My mother said I was probably right. She said she would go to the firehouse on West 161st Street and speak with a man who is especially trained for this type situation. "He comes with a powder that is white. He puts it on everyone's hands and when he does it to the arsonist, the powder turns blue." At that juncture, I stood up and cried out, "I did it." In confessing, I had to tell my mother how I lit the paper. She brought me into the bathroom to witness the charred ruins and told me, as only a loving mother could, the potential effects of such behavior. I brought on the tears and my mother said she'd tell my father and ask him for amnesty for me because it was my birthday. She apparently did a good job. When my father came home from work, he went into the bathroom after my mother whispered to him. He must have realized that this had to be kept quiet. The landlord lived in the next apartment. My dad came into the living room and grunted, "Don't ever do anything like that again," I said I wouldn't and that was the end of that.

Saturday morning was a thrill in those days. We used to go to the Audubon Movie Theatre. My mother would give my brother, Larry, a half dollar and enough change for us to buy popcorn. For just two bits we saw a triple feature, thirty cartoons, eight vaudeville acts and we even got a chance on a bicycle. Oh yeah, we also got a comic book, saw a serial which was continued each week and was given a free dish plate. We'd go into the movie house at about noon and when we got out, it was dark and time for dinner.

My parents took church seriously. My brothers and I went to Saint Rose of Lima Grammar School. You were obligated to go to the nine o'clock Mass on Sundays and join your class. Your teacher would peer over everyone's shoulder and if you moved the wrong way you were advised of it with any icy stare. An appropriate sentence was invoked on Monday morning.

It was interesting to note that altar boys could serve Mass on weekdays at the church, which was adjacent to the school. It would be an automatic and acceptable excuse to come late for class. The only problem was you had to learn the Latin prayers. Johnny Coffey's uncle dropped out of the seminary and taught Johnny and me. We knew our Latin cold, but we didn't know what to do during Mass or when to do it. Furthermore, we didn't know when to invoke each Latin response. We must have waited a year before anyone was interested enough to train us. Then, one day, the youngest priest in the parish, Father Costello, said to the two of us, "You're on!" We had about five minutes to get ready. It was almost impossible to button the cassocks we wore. There must have been forty buttons. There was also the job of selecting a surplus that fit, but we made it. We approached the altar like pros. We knelt down and Father Costello started to utter the prayers. We were at a loss. We didn't know when to say the Latin, so whenever he spoke, we responded with a Latin response. The only problem was that we ran out of Latin after the first five minutes. At one point, we knew we had to move the large book, the one on the heavy stand, to the other side of the altar. This was done simultaneously as the cloth that covered the chalice was moved as well. We had to crisscross coming down the steps. We both stumbled over each other and the round book support went rumbling down the main aisle of the long church. After the Mass, Father Costello said he thought we were trained and was apologetic for our sad performance. He said he'd arrange for training and told us to report to the portion of the church where we vested on Saturday. When we got there, the biggest altar boy with his buddies were waiting. They said we had to be initiated and had an instrument that worked in a manner similar to a tazer gun. He zapped me first and it really hurt. I kicked him as he dropped the tazer like weapon, and I clobbered him with it. At that point, we ran, yelling that we'd tell our parents. We had to come back the next week. This time, they were afraid to do anything in case they got in trouble. They still acted like bullies, but the leader of the pack sported a black eye. That was a great shot I had at him!

I was one of the smallest kids in my class. The bullies loved to pick on me. They loved making fun of my thick glasses but I usually mustered up the courage to protect myself despite of the fear I felt. Learning how to box lefty helped and the bigger kids knew I'd give them a battle. Therefore, they found someone else to be their punching bag. Why can't adults solve this problem? Children shouldn't be pestered by their peers! Bullies are maggots! "Bad luck to them!"

Johnny and I served many a Mass. The retired pastor was known as "Doctor Mahoney" and said Mass on the side altar. He was too old and frail to navigate the five or six steps of the main altar. It was truly an honor, holding his arm so he wouldn't fall. He couldn't see well and used a prayer book with extremely large fonts. He must have been ninety. Father Costello had a great rapport with all the altar boys. We always wished that he'd be the celebrant of the Mass. He eventually became a bishop. There were also Fathers O'Brien and Pregenser. They always made it a point to thank you for serving. Father Murray was a different story. He was a pain in the ass. Why would a guy like this ever become a priest? We figured that he probably went to the seminary to avoid the draft. He was a first-class picky grouch. He also reeked from alcohol more often than not.

Saint Rose of Lima was a school where the Dominican Nuns ruled and we received an outstanding education. Fear was a great teacher. They invented Limbo and knew the answers to everything. In learning the corporal works of mercy, I asked Sister Andrew what was meant by, "Harbor the harborless." She said, "Just memorize it." Everyone sat at attention and learned. Each student was responsible for his or her own desk. To mark it up called for a death sentence and restitution from the parents. Frequent inspections insured that the wood was clear from writing and the inkwell was filled with royal blue washable, Sheffield ink. They prepared us for high school and taught us in the ways of our religion. Looking back, I loved them for being so devoted to their vocation.

Graduation Day in 1951 was a memorable experience. I was given a maroon, plastic portable radio, which was the recent rave. It weighed about fifteen pounds because of the old fashioned battery. Whenever you took it to the beach, sand got in it and adhered to the speaker like a magnet.

My Uncle Paddy took me to Florida that summer. We traveled in his brand new Ford sedan. There was my uncle, my Aunt Liz, Betty, Jimmy and Tommy. The trip for me was an awakening to a new world I had never seen before. The ferry at the southern tip of New Jersey was replaced by the Delaware Memorial Bridge and there were no interstate highways. But that's not what I'm talking about. Black people were abused in a manner that I didn't know existed. They were restricted in public places and ridiculed by sign postings such as "Whites Only." Also, "Negroes" were destined never to frequent the same areas as whites. The roads bore Burma Shave ads that were humorous, and Black Chain Gangs that will forever be etched on my mind. Now I knew what it was like when my mother told me how she felt as a new Irish immigrant when signs in the butcher shops read, "Cured at Lourdes." I had felt proud as an American when we won the war but my spirits about our country were dampened by the fact that we allowed the black people to be oppressed, abused and victimized. The trip was documented with an Argus Camera that my Aunt Annie Maguire gave me when I graduated. Those images are reminders of an ugly time in our history.

Paddy's aunt had a home in West Palm Beach and it was beautiful. His son, Jimmy, and I scouted the area together. It was on this trip that I discovered oppression in our country. Many people from down South referred to northerners as red necks. They not only looked down on "Negroes," but on us as well. They were still fighting the Civil War. Never before did I live in an area where there was a class distinction and I was at the top of the food chain. It was strange playing the role of a little, rich kid and it didn't feel good. It almost felt as though I joined a culture unwillingly that was morally wrong. Because of this uneasiness, I couldn't enjoy myself as much as I pretended I did for my uncle's sake. It must have been great living in Palm Beach, lolly gagging in the parks, boating and shooting hammerhead sharks with a rifle at the end of the piers and going to the beach everyday; but how does anyone live with the stigma of witnessing the suffering of so many. You could see that the Negroes were disadvantaged, lacked a proper education and were forced to kiss the rear ends of the pompous, grit devouring, spoiled rebels.

On my way back and forth to New York City, I had my first glimpse of military life. Convoys passed us on the roads several times.

We avoided the speed trap in Ludowici, Georgia. It was publicized in the New York papers. This town had a man one flight up in a hotel room with a traffic control remote. When a New York, New Jersey or Pennsylvania car approached the intersection, he turned the light red so quickly you couldn't stop in time. A cop's car pulled the violator over immediately, hauled the owner off to court and bail had to be posted. They ripped off all these northerners. This town projected the attitude of most southerners and no one did a thing about it.

The worst thing I saw was the Black Chain Gangs. They were all linked together and a police officer stood over them in the sweltering heat with a loaded shotgun as they dug away. It reminded me of the Jews who were persecuted during the war. To think that we thought the 1951 Ford was hot without air conditioning!

It made me wonder why I never heard about the miserable living conditions down South. Although I felt guilty, there was little I could do about it at the age of fourteen; but I promised myself that I'd never discriminate against anyone, and if I ever had children, I'd discourage them against being so narrow-minded and bigoted.

In those days, television made its debut in the home of America. While the rest of the world watched Milton Berle, my family watched Bishop Sheehan. We also watched Father Payton who preached, "The family that prays together, stays together."

On Friday night we went to the corner luncheonette. We ordered a chocolate malted and watched the wrestling matches. We couldn't order a second malted because we didn't have the money.

Well, summer was almost over and the next step or stumbling block in my life would be high school.

2

LIFE AS A TEENAGER

During the fall of that year, a great decision had to be made in my life. However, it was an easy one to be made. Applications were sent to various high schools and I was accepted to several including Bishop Dubois which was on West 152nd Street and Amsterdam Avenue. The tuition was comparatively cheap at Dubois. It was ten dollars a month and its reputation was good. My brother, Larry, was already a student there and had managed to eke by. They had an unbendable policy. If you failed a subject, you went to Summer School. If you failed there, you were expelled, and if you failed two subjects you were also out. Then you had no choice but to finish high school at George Washington, which was the local public school. The freshman year at Bishop Dubois had a hundred and fifty enrollees and the senior year had about seventy. There were a little more than three hundred students in the school and there was no gym or recreational facilities to talk about. There was only a schoolyard where basketball was played during lunch. The basketball team, however, was one of the best in the city. Every indication was that Bishop DuBois would be a scholastic challenge. There was quite a difference in schools considering quality of education and discipline. Also, Bishop Dubois was a long walk and George Washington was a bus ride.

My parents dictated that I go to Bishop Dubois. The faculty consisted of priests and Marist Brothers. I sensed that there would be a radical change in lifestyle. It was a step in my life that I dreaded. I wasn't afraid of the schoolwork but I feared being bullied. It wouldn't be any fun being one of the smallest kids in the class. Past experience was enough to warn me that I'd be picked on as soon as I set my foot on school grounds. However, despite sleepless nights of worry, the day of reckoning arrived. It should have been consoling that I had an older brother, but he was a firm believer in fending for yourself. Trying to express my concerns to him was useless; he merely laughed and told me I'd get my butt kicked.

My first day of high school was one of the most memorable ones in my life. As I arrived at the school, Brother Henry Joe who always held a clipboard greeted me. If you were late, he'd tell you to report for "jug." This meant you'd have to see him at the end of the school day and spend a minimum of two hours with him. He'd give you an assignment and you were prohibited from doing your homework. He was the Dean of Discipline. He spoke with a Spanish accent and during lunch hour; he had students report to him when they were in trouble, and others who wanted to learn subjects that were not part of the curriculum. It was a mistake to ever comment that we should learn Spanish instead of French because you'd involuntarily give up your lunch and learn Spanish without getting school credit. He also had many students at noon who felt they should have typing classes. If you took your fingers off the home positions to take a bite out of your sandwich, you'd pay the sacrifice of getting smacked in the head. In any case, as I entered the school, Brother Henry Joe told me, along with the other freshmen, to report to the auditorium. As I arrived there, several students had arrived ahead of me and were chewing the fat. In a friendly manner, I interrupted and asked them if they were freshman as well. Sure enough, the tallest one pushed me deliberately and told me to take a hike. It was the same old crap all over again. I gave him a drop kick, which I rehearsed all summer. My shoes landed in his diaphragm and winded him. He grunted but hauled back with his right to deliver a haymaker. My defense mechanisms kicked in and I ducked, getting as low to the ground as I could. His body went over mine as I struggled to stand. He went topsy-turvy and landed on his head. I clenched my fists and said, "Did you have enough?" With that, a warning was heard that Brother Henry Joe was on his way to give us Orientation. We all found the nearest seat. My foe had a red protrusion on his forehead, a tear in his eye and a badly bruised ego. I prayed that this would be a fight that ended after one round. It was a great thing that so many of the new students knew I'd stand my ground.

Orientation included being given a schedule of classes. This included all subjects and times. There were no options or alternatives. We were told that everyone was expected to do at least three hours of homework a night.

The rest of the day was spent meeting my new teachers. Father Fallon was the Religion teacher. He resembled a movie star. He spoke in a low pitch and appeared to be a saintly character. In time, students took advantage of his good nature. He never became discouraged as he constantly looked upward. He always appeared as though he was at prayer. He was a man who had a positive effect on my life. He was a great promoter of the Blessed Mother and encouraged me to pray to her. I admired him for being able to put up with the smart asses in my class and maintaining his cool at all times. His goodness made the kids causing disruptions in his class appear downright evil to me. He was such a nice guy and great teacher; I always tried my best in his class.

Father Kowski was the Latin teacher. He was raised on the tugboats in New York Harbor. His brother was a Deputy Police Chief and he became the New York Police Chaplain at a later time. On occasion he smoked cigars during class and a student was designated to stand guard in case the Principal, Monsignor Buckley arrived in the hallway unexpectedly. He wore a ring, which he used to rap you in the forehead if you failed to answer a question relating to your homework assignment. He was a gruff character but you couldn't help but respect him. Furthermore, he projected a true enjoyment in being a priest. His buddy and fellow priest, Father Cahier, was cut from the same cloth. These two men gave the school character and charisma. They were men of God who fought their way to a vocation by preaching the gospel in ways that God reserved only for them and they did it well.

Brother George was truly French; all six foot four of him. I can recall the day when he asked me how to say "United States" in French. Well, I studied my vocabulary words and responded Etats-Unis. He charged at me and gave me the correct pronunciation along with several punches. If it wasn't for his cassock, I think I would have cut the legs out from under him. Who the hell gave him the idea that he should punch out a student, especially one who studied his homework. Furthermore, the spelling told me that all the French were mispronouncing the word for the United States.

I suspect he disliked my New York hybrid accent with Irish-American flair. As my father used to say, "Bad luck to him!" I knew that I'd never go to France after knowing Brother George. Again, I wondered why a man would dedicate himself to a vocation of teaching children and then abuse them. He certainly struck me, but not as a follower of Christ.

Getting back to that first day, the last class was Science. As I entered the laboratory an alien feeling came upon me. I prayed that I was wrong.

The Science teacher's name was Brother Thomas. He had a unique style to his teaching. He was always two steps ahead of everyone and loved to surprise you. On that day, he gave us a quiz. I couldn't believe it. It was the first day of school. The test consisted of fifty questions, each worth two points. All the answers were true, false or fill ins. It was about the hardest test I had ever taken in my life. I hardly knew any of the answers. I was devastated! That night, I couldn't sleep. It was my feeling that I didn't have the brains to finish high school. For the first time in my life, I felt I was dumb. I shared my feelings with my family. My mom was sympathetic and said she was sure things would get better. My dad said, "Study, Lad!" My brother, Frank, stayed awake with me for hours, but finally succumbed to sleep. I didn't talk to Larry about it.

The next morning, I was afraid to go to school for the first time in my life. Furthermore, I think I slept only a couple hours. It was my desire that Science class would never come but it did. Each class began with a prayer as this one did. Finally, Brother Thomas said, "Who is Mister Niland?" I raised my hand knowing well that I was about to be verbally flogged and humiliated. Brother Thomas acknowledged me and said that I scored a forty on the quiz, "Forty out of a hundred!" The class roared in prolonged laughter. The cackles seemed to last for ten minutes as Brother Thomas finally interrupted them and stated that I had the highest mark in the class. He proceeded to call each by name, announcing how poorly each individual did. I thought his method of teaching stunk, but I was so relieved hearing the final test scores of the other students.

Many times in later life, I wondered what he hoped to accomplish by such shenanigans. However, his class was bearable. He also taught Biology but he scared me away from Chemistry when the choice was given to me in later grades.

My class was the first one to graduate from the new gym. After four years of education at Bishop Dubois, I felt knowledgeable in the society of the time. Those high school years were some of the best ones in my life.

My buddy, Dooley, was a class behind me. He never worked during his high school years. His family went to Breezy Point in Queens, NY for the summer. He was ashamed that he wasn't in any school activities. He said that there would be nothing written in the yearbook under his picture when he graduated so he joined the baseball team. He was a natural athlete but never took the trouble to learn the game. However, he had natural talent that couldn't be ignored and was a first stringer on the team. He was known for his ability to hit. Once, our team was playing a meaningful game on its schedule. We were tied one to one in the bottom of the last inning with a runner on third and one out when Vinny came to the plate. The signal was given for a suicide bunt. He didn't understand what was going on. The pitch came in and the runner from third charged the plate, Vinny swung the bat and narrowly missed his head. Naturally, the runner was tagged out. The coach and the team were livid. On the next pitch, he knocked the ball over the fence for a walk off victory. It just goes to show you, a win makes errors hard to remember. Results seem to be the only thing that matters in this world.

Our days down Riverside Drive were numbered. I got a job after school working at a dairy on West 165th Street and St. Nicholas Avenue. I got out of school at 3:00 p.m. and reported to work at 4:00 p.m. I stocked the shelves, helped to unload trucks, worked at the cheese counter and on Saturday, I worked from 7:00 a.m. to 7:00 p.m. On occasion, I helped at the cashier's counter. I loaded the bags and tallied the charges by writing on one of the brown bags. The salary wasn't bad; I earned $22.00 per week, made tips and kept the deposits from the bottles. It was frustrating to carry a large order of groceries a long distance and have the customer give you a tip of several bottles, which you now had to carry the same distance to get the refund. The larger bottles were good for a nickel and the smaller ones two cents. The neighborhood started to go downhill in those years. It seemed that the poorer people were the best tippers. I delivered groceries to the elite on Riverside Drive and to the Brownstones on Edgecombe Avenue as well as to the poor in the six-story walk-ups closer to the store. Some of the orders I delivered were rather unique. Every Saturday a small box of refreshment drinks were delivered to the guy who ran the numbers racket. There was no OTB (City sponsored off track betting). Upon delivery, Sal gave me a dollar from the stacks of bills numbering thirty or forty on his kitchen table. A dollar was a great tip. I figured it was intended to shut me up as well. One of his pansies used to walk the avenues, stop in all the stores and see his regulars. The usual contribution was a quarter and that was usually for a boxed number meaning any combination of the three numbers selected.

There was a very wealthy black woman, Mrs. Pierre, who lived in a Brownstone. On the outside, it resembled all the other homes in the area but inside it was a showplace. Each room was paneled in different kinds of wood. The décor was out of "Better Homes." She also gave me a dollar. I never saw her husband but she was beautiful and always dressed to kill, never casually.

There was a Spanish woman who was always very cheerful when she entered the store. I personally helped her because I stocked the shelves and knew where the "Goya" food was stashed. It was always the largest delivery because there were so many people living in that apartment. Despite the size of the order, it was another buck I could count on.

The first week I worked that job was a tiring one. When I came home, my dad told me there was a tradition in the family. A son's first week's pay was given to his father. I figured it was a put on and I wouldn't play into his hands, so I reached into my pocket and gave him my full salary (twenty-two dollars.) He said thanks and kept the money. I thought for sure that he would be giving it back but that never happened. There was an important lesson to be leaned, but I never figured out what it was.

I did, however, learn an important lesson at my workplace after I became very knowledgeable about the job. The owner, Sam, asked if I could work long hours with him for a week so he could send his wife on a vacation. He said he'd pay overtime. I didn't know exactly what that meant but I assumed it was time and a half. I agreed to work from 7:00 a.m. to 7:00 p.m. for six days since school was closed for the summer. In my mind, I projected a paycheck of over $100. I worked hard every hour that week. I did what Rose, Sam's wife, normally did and managed to do my job as well. At the end of the week, Rose returned from her jaunt to Florida with her son. He was a despicable character who worked for General Motors and

bragged how he left at least one screw out of every Chevy's glove com-
partment on the assembly line. Rose came to the back of the store where
I was and acknowledged the good job I did when she was gone. She was
always the one who figured out my pay. She started her computation with
saying that my regular salary was $22.00 and my normal hourly pay was
a dollar something, but Sam and she had a small store and they couldn't
afford paying me the same hourly rate for the numerous hours I worked.
There was no mention of an overtime rate of pay. Now I felt scammed
and couldn't concentrate on the diatribe she was insulting me with. I was
pissed. She gave me a note to collect fifty dollars from Sam at the register. I
was too angry to say anything to her. I went to Sam, gave him the note and
he gave me fifty dollars. He smiled and said "That's quite a paycheck you've
earned!" I said, Find yourself another flunky, I quit." This was big business
oppressing me on a small-time basis. I said to myself, "They aren't going to
get away with this. Sam is a first class maggot and bad luck to him!"

My mother was a regular customer and had no knowledge of my quitting. She was surprised to hear of it when she went there to shop. She
came home and asked me the details. She was very loving but had that
instilled fear of an immigrant. She asked me to reconsider and said that
Sam would give me back the job. Rather than get my mother involved, I
told her that Sam could discuss it if he came to me. My mother said she'd
tell him what I said. There were three opinions prevalent in this matter. My
mother wanted me working and off the streets. Sam wanted to rip me off
and I refused to be screwed. I did honest work and deserved honest pay. I
was intent on filing charges against him with the Labor Board if he didn't
remedy his transgression.

Having thought through what I had to do when Sam came, I met him
on the sidewalk outside my apartment house. He asked what I wanted. I
told him I wanted to be paid retroactively at the rate of $1.75 per hour
and for the week of controversy time and a half. Furthermore, he would
pay me in the future by keeping track of my hours. His wife would not be
involved. He smiled and said he was a small store and couldn't afford my
demands but perhaps we could reach a compromise. I saw where this was
going and said there were no other options on the table. I decided to get
a lawyer if my demands weren't met. He violated child labor laws, and I
would teach him and his wife that they can't treat a dedicated worker as

a peon. Through the grapevine, I heard that he had replaced me with a teenager who was caught robbing from him. Again, Sam said, "Surely we could work something out." I told him if he walked away without agreeing to my terms, the die was cast. He reluctantly agreed.

After that, I lost all respect for him. The store was divided in half. Sam Nugent was the butcher and co-renter. They shared the rent. Sam Nugent owned over twenty lake-front cabins in Chester, New York. His wife was extremely overweight and their son was as well. He always ranted and raved that he'd like to treat me to a day in the country. Finally, I agreed. When I arrived, he had plans carefully worked out. He wanted me to clean out a barn-like building loaded with crap. There must have been enough work for two men. His son was too busy to help because he was studying his German for school. Two employees claimed he was the cheapest bastard they ever worked for. They said that he told them that he was going to get someone to clean the building out. I said to myself, "He's another guy that's trying to take advantage of me," so I decided to take him up on the day in the country that he promised me. I stripped to my underwear and dove into the refreshing lake. I found a large inner tube and was floating in paradise when I heard the desperate calls of Sam Nugent. I pretended I didn't hear him. I barely kept from laughing as I uttered to myself, "Bad luck to him!" Finally, I came to shore in time for a dinner, which consisted of burned steak. I suspected that the meat was old and would have had to be thrown out if we didn't eat it. Sam said he was counting on me to help him. I told him I was counting on a leisurely day in the country. I couldn't resist looking at him eyeball-to-eyeball and saying, "You brought me up here under false pretenses." He was speechless for the rest of dinner and during the trip home.

The two Sams didn't get along and their poor relationship peaked during the Jewish holidays. Sam Brudner would take a rope and put it down the middle of the store. He would instruct me to inform his customers that he was closed for the Jewish holidays. They would then ask Sam Nugent if he was Jewish. He'd say yes, but he didn't celebrate the holidays. I got paid while I sat on my duff at the cashier's counter.

After the incident I endured when they tried to hustle me out of pay, I never did anything to save them money. I merely did what I had to do. When I saw that they were running out of stock on a particular product, I said nothing. I didn't get paid to take inventory. If I saw someone stealing from one of the shelves, I did nothing. I didn't get paid to do security. This is the price oppressors must pay and their attitude towards their workers eventually puts them out of business. "Good Riddance!"

During those years, I gave my mom $22.00 a week plus anything else I earned for working extra hours. I used my tips to hustle in the poolroom. The manager taught me how to play three-cushion billiards. Knowing how to play this game and doing well at it made me an unbeatable player at straight pool. I banked another $20.00 a week from my winnings and also paid my tuition of $10.00 a month at Bishop Dubois.

About once a week, usually on Sunday after Mass, I'd go with Dooley to Riverside Drive. We'd frequently run into Jackie Ahern. He was a nice guy who was a little older than we and in peak physical shape. His father was the superintendent of a building off Amsterdam Avenue. He also went to Saint Rose of Lima at one time. From what I heard, a nun made him dance in one of the annual fund-raising school plays and someone from Lincoln Center recognized his raw talent and paid his way to a professional dance career. He spent hours at a time working out on the chinning and parallel bars. He was good enough to show Vinny and me many of the tricks and proper way to train as it was taught to him. He had amazing skill. He could stay in the "L" position for several minutes from the chinning bar before going into a perfect "U" which astonished both Vinny and me. He was the first person I ever knew who wore contact lenses. He was preparing for a movie and was practicing to throw a dagger as he had been taught. He showed us how he came to be so accurate. He said he was going to be in a movie, "Seven Brides for Seven Brothers." Because his name, Jackie Ahern, was considered blasé, his manager had him take the name Jacques D'Amboise. He was a great guy and I'm sure he never realized how much his training tips meant to me. Although, I was lean, I had grown to six foot and was strong. My forte was the fact that I had endurance, strength and still knew all the tricks I used when I was small.

My grades in school were satisfactory and my reading skills had improved greatly, despite the fact that many of my book reports were based on what I read in "Classic Comics."

My first girlfriend was a girl named Helen. We used to go to the movies and make out once a week. Eventually, I had puppy love for Joan. We used to date regularly and she was the girl that I took to my high school prom. She wore my school ring visibly around her neck. It was a sign for the world that we were going steady. However, we got tired of each other. The other girls in my life at the time were two German sisters. At first I dated Helga and later, Inge. Their mother was an immigrant and treated her daughters as fraulines. My buddy, Johnny Coffey, and I dated Inge at different times. Johnny never worked. He went to a different high school than I, but we remained very close. Vinny used to tell us about the wonderful girls he dated but we never saw them. Vinny had a way with girls and he was good looking. There was no reason to think that he was anything other than straight.

Vinny's oldest brother, Tommy, graduated with honors from Bishop Dubois. He surprised everyone when he enlisted in the Marine Corps. Vinny raved about how his brother went through the challenge of rigorous training at Parris Island and painted a picture of the Marine Corps that I found to be alluring.

Sadly, Vinny's brother, as he told me, got messed up in a beach landing in Korea. He was sent back to the states to a Veteran's Hospital. In time, I felt that the truth was more that he cracked up mentally in basic training. Vinny visited him often. He was depressed that his brother had mental problems and he studied psychiatry and discussed it often with me. It sounded as though Vinny was going over the deep edge and there was nothing I could do about it. He had to analyze everything no matter how simple it was and then tell me why certain things happen according to Freud. You could no longer have an intelligent conversation with him.

We were still living in the armpit of New York City. It was commonplace to be mugged if you were an adult with money. I recall my Uncle Tommy was beaten and left for dead one night coming home from work. He was taken to Mother Cabrini Hospital on Edgecombe Avenue. When I heard about this terrible incident, I rushed to his side. He was lying on a cot in a ward at the hospital. He was beaten to a pulp. They took his tools (he was a carpenter) and his money. He was sorely outnumbered. It was no longer safe to get off the subway at 161st Street on the IND Subway Line.

Once my dad was having a few beers at Bradley's Bar and Grill. An Irish immigrant, half his age, had evil words with him. My dad was feeling a buzz and mouthed off at him. This young greenhorn beat my dad ferociously. He knocked out a tooth and left him with two shiners. Dad wouldn't say who did it. My brother, Larry, and I went to Bradley's Bar and asked around. My dad was respected and several of his friends told us who inflicted this beating on him. We found out where the culprit lived and went to his apartment. It was like a rooming house. We weren't invited in, but I noticed a figure hugging the hallway so he wouldn't be seen. We had no choice but to leave. We went back to the Bradley's and asked when this Irishman usually comes in. We were told at 7:00 p.m. We were waiting for him and gave him the beating of his life. He spent that summer in the park outside his building in casts and crutches. I'd stop by and taunt him when I was going to church, which was opposite the park. When I entered church I felt like a hypocrite. I kept asking God to help me square myself away. I knew I should have felt sorrow, but I loved my dad and had no other way to express the sadness I felt. I knew anger wasn't the answer, but I just couldn't let this young man walk away unscathed from the terrible wrong he had done. My father was upset over what we did as well and also felt responsible for our actions. Part of the problem was living in a rotten area. Living in a cesspool is a losing formula for everyone.

It seemed to be a gift from God. My uncle Mike, my dad's brother who also worked for the Transit Authority told my dad that he had forty thousand dollars in his pension. He found out that he was dying and wanted my father to have the money when he died. When I heard of this, I thought it was our way out of the gutter. I didn't know if my parents saved a penny. They were very secretive about their money. The only thing I knew was that my mother kept cash in the leg of our old-fashioned bathroom tub.

Uncle Mike died. He had been married at one time and I suspected that he married his wife because she was pregnant. Their marriage was short lived and I saw Mike infrequently. Although it sounds cold, he used to hurt me when I was small. He pinched and taunted me and I hated the stench of booze from his breath.

I wonder how many children are treated roughly by their uncles, in front of their parents. Little people have big feelings. Their parents should always be vigilant and take the appropriate action necessary. This is the responsibility of a parent.

My father decided to send the money to my Aunt Bridie in Ireland. He had asked Mike to do this, but he wouldn't listen. It seems Bridie had several children, and in my father's opinion, needed the money more than we. A couple weeks later, he received a letter from the parish priest in Ireland saying to send Bridie the rest of the money. "There surely is more." Well there was. My dad paid for Mike's funeral expenses and for a tombstone. He was buried at Gate of Heaven Cemetery in Hawthorne, New York. After that, he had three hundred dollars; that is, until he went into a bar that Mike frequented. The bartender showed my dad how Mike stiffed him for $100. Naturally, my dad wanted to keep my uncle's good name in perpetuity so he honored the IOU. Then my dad was summoned to court when Mike's ex-wife came out of the woodwork. The judge demanded that he give her half of what was left which was $100. He said he'd rather go to jail. The judge said he could accommodate him so my father gave her the money.

My dad was notorious for making weird decisions. Once, he and a drinking buddy, wanted to buy a chicken farm. My mother killed his dream when she told him she wasn't going to feed the chickens and collect their eggs. This scheme was never mentioned again.

My loving aunt and godmother, Nonie, came over from Ireland at the turn of the century. She invested in land in Rahway, New Jersey. She was now in her nineties and couldn't afford the taxes. My dad took a ride, inspected the land and peed on it. He let the land go despite its value. I pleaded with him to pay the taxes or give it to me but he said it wasn't worth it.

Witnessing such magnanimous decisions was frustrating. I had only four hundred dollars in the bank and my father's attitude was, "The hell with college – get a Civil Service job." At the time, college loans weren't available for me, and I was probably going to be drafted in the near future. Dad was a union man and fought with Mike Quill and the transit workers for rights. He felt that was all the security one needed.

Graduation should have been something to celebrate. It was for my parents because they never finished more than two years of school. However, they were self-educated. My mother was well read and my dad was good at math. This helped him with his job as a mason on the subways. For me, I was accepted into several colleges and I formally accepted Iona in New Rochelle. Unfortunately, Manhattan College did not accept me. It was my hope that I could travel there by subway. With New Rochelle, it meant a bus to West 125th Street, another cross-town bus to Park Avenue and then the Metro train to Main Street in New Rochelle. Then, I had to walk about a mile. This school commute, working part time, hours of study and a nagging father was too much. After six months, I decided it was time to enlist in the service. After all, when I got out, there was the GI Bill. I could return to school at that time. Furthermore, I'd get out of the terrible area where I lived.

My brother, Larry, tried to enlist in the Navy. This was a life-long ambition of his, but it was determined he had Diabetes and he was 4F. He knew something was wrong because he was constantly thirsty and lost a great deal of weight over a short period of time.

If I joined the Navy, I visualized being stranded at sea. I'd never forget my raft trip to New York Harbor and the feeling of being marooned. The Air Force didn't appeal to me. When I was at Iona, I inquired about being a Platoon leader in the Marine Corps and they told me I could never be a pilot because of my poor eyesight. I couldn't picture being on the ground while others in the air shared all the thrills and excitement. Then I asked myself if I could make it in the Marine Corps. Apparently, this was the challenge! My buddy, Johnny, and I decided to go into the Corps together. There was a delay because my father and mother wouldn't sign for me; I was seventeen, and so I went into the Marine Corps on my eighteenth birthday. The exodus wasn't glorious. My dad was ticked at me and we argued for several days. His good-bye refrain was like this, "Do what you want son!" That morning, I embarked on the Eighth Avenue Express with my tail between my legs. It was a terrible feeling leaving under these circumstances. My mom had tears in her eyes.

Johnny's folks weren't too happy with him either. It was February 1956 and the Korean Conflict was over. We wondered if there would be enough excitement to satisfy us in the Marine Corps. One thing we knew, we were about to find out.

3

A FEW GOOD MEN

As I rode that train, I wondered for the first time if I made the right decision but I knew there was no turning back. Johnny must have felt the same way because we kept assuring each other that we'd make it.

We reported to a public room somewhere at Penn Station and got sworn into the Marine Corps. Up to this point, we had only seen recruit Sergeants. One of them was to accompany us on our rail trip to Parris Island, South Carolina for basic training. However, we never saw him on the trip. He must have wiggled his way into first class.

All the recruits mingled immediately. We obviously had a lot in common. One guy from Brooklyn had his mom and dad there to say goodbye. It made me wish that mine were there as well. His nickname was, "Tiny." He must have weighed two hundred and fifty pounds. One guy named Krumrod was a motorcycle enthusiast and wore a black, leather jacket. He struck me as a guy who liked to fight. He had very long hair. One guy, Leo, had his serious embrace with the girl he was leaving behind broken up by the recruiter.

Finally, we boarded the train. We had a few beers packed for the trip and because they served booze on the train, we saw no problems in having a few drinks before we entered military life. When we got to Washington, D.C., we were hooked up to a train that the old railroad buffs liked to travel on. It was called the Palmlander; or at least that's what I was told. It was the same train that was in the Laurel and Hardy movies with upper and lower sleepers. The drinking laws on the train changed from state to state, and we became familiar with the rules an hour before we crossed state lines.

Despite the rocking and noise, we arrived sober in Yamasee, South Carolina; the gateway to Parris Island. As we disembarked, we were guided to a staging area and lined up in a relaxed single file. Finally, a sharply dressed Marine with a clipboard approached us. He started to give us directions in his rebel drawl. I remembered the accent from my previous trip down South. He stood in front of one of the recruits and mumbled, "Swallow that glob!" His instructions were undecipherable and prompted this response, "Take the shit out of your mouth." In response to the recruit's arrogance, the Sergeant stuck him in the eye with his pencil. You could hear the graphite puncture the eye socket. The recruit grabbed his eye and screamed in pain. He fell to the ground in agony. The Marine then said to one and all, this will happen to you, if you chew gum in the Corps. An ambulance was dispatched and arrived in no time to take away our first training casualty.

We then loaded "cattle cars," olive drab contraptions that resembled a bus. It also was similar to a semi-trailer and was obviously used to transport military personnel. We were off to our destination but we couldn't get over the incident we just witnessed. Few words were spoken and most of us sat in total disbelief over what had just happened.

As we disembarked from the troop carrier, there were three loud Marines who introduced themselves to us as our Drill Instructors (DIs). They were absolutely in our face and everyone was scared shit: at least I was. The older man was Staff Sergeant Banks. We knew his rank because he told us. He had three stripes with a 'rocker' under them. He also had four 'hash' marks; smaller stripes on the sleeves. Each hash mark represented four years of service, which I learned at a later time. He was decorated with many ribbons; each representing a medal that he was awarded. I didn't know what they were for but determined at a later time that they were citations for the various campaigns he had participated in. He was dressed in a meticulous manner. His shoes had a mirror shine. We all looked liked bums in the company of these three guys.

The Corporal (two stripes) said nothing but also had an ominous presence and was well dressed but lacked all the ribbons. He had no hash marks. His name was Corporal Bailey.

The other man was the best-dressed guy that I ever saw in my life and he knew it. You could see everything reflecting on his shoes. His shirt was tailor-made and showed off his muscular torso. His belt buckle glittered in the bright, warm sun. He took command as he yelled at us for being stupid, sloppy, and ignorant. For the first time I heard the word "maggot" to describe our demeanor. He also sported several ribbons and presented himself as one mean machine of a Marine. His name was Sergeant Gonzalez. He said we didn't have to know his first name because he'd beat the shit out of us if we ever used it. He double-timed us to an area where we were to receive government issued clothes. We then had a rendezvous with guys from down South before this occurred; they also became members of Platoon 60.

When we entered this storehouse building, there were Marines dressed in what is referred to as "utilities." This is what is worn usually during a workday.

We quickly learned the names used for wearing apparel. A "blouse" was a utility top and "trousers" were pants, A "hat" was referred to as a cover. Shoes that came up to your ankle were called "boon dockers" and the ones that rested on your shins were "boots." Even the underwear had specific names. Underpants were called "skivvies" and the shirts were referred to as "skivvy shirts." At a later time we were issued barrack caps, and other caps which were to be worn only on base. Dress clothes in olive drab and tropical colors were also issued later in training. At Parris Island, no one tastes a lick of liberty and every twitch of your body is observed, analyzed and closely scrutinized.

We lined up at counters and a demeaning voice would shout "What size?" You'd yell the size and he'd pelt you with the clothes. The guy in front of me was asked what size shoe he wore. He responded, "Any size will do, sir?" The Corporal jumped the counter to whack him for being a wise guy, but he saw that he was barefooted. The Corporal then asked if he ever owned a pair of shoes. He said, "No. sir." He then asked where he was from. He said, "I'm a Kentucky volunteer, sir." After getting our first military clothing issue, we loaded everything as it was given to us in a sea bag. We then double-timed again in the hot sun for about a mile to a gym- like building. Guys were falling by the wayside as we traveled. Each time they'd fall out, they were kicked, shoved and punched. All of them were instantly cured and got back into ranks; it was sheer fear that brought me to my destination.

This area was loaded with sailors who acted very effeminate. We had to strip, put our civilian clothes in a box, address the parcel to send it home and stand at attention in our skivvies. A despicable guy in a sailor suit then came around with a violet marker and painted a number on our chest. The guy who marked my chest smiled and said, "You're number seven!" This smart ass spoke with a deliberate lisp. His type apparently put in for duty at Parris Island to be with the Marine recruits. The DIs knew they tormented the troops and they found it laughable. These swabbies (sailors) then conducted basic medical tests. At this time, several recruits figured they wanted out. One recruit was asked to read an eye chart. He said, "Sir, I can't see the chart!" the DI said go ahead, "You pass!" He retorted, "But sir, I can't see the chart." His response was, "This is a hearing test stupid!"

The sailors only did what the DIs told them to do and nothing more. We then received inoculations before the DIs demanded the sailors leave the building.

We all stood in fear and at attention or at least I did. They demonstrated what the positions of attention were and demanded that we never forget them. The three DI s went to the first guy in formation and asked him, "What is your name?" He responded with his name and the Drill Instructor beat him to the ground. He then gave us the ground rules. He said you must first request permission from the Sergeant to speak. If permission is granted, you must refer to yourself as "Private" and refer to the other person by his rank; he then proceeded to the next recruit. He said, "What's your name?" The reply was, "Private Tomchak requests permission to speak to the Drill Instructor. "I thought he passed the scrutiny," but he got punched and was told, you must say "Sir" before and after. The next recruit was a guy I met from the armpit of the Bronx. His name was Ed Parsley. The DI asked him the usual question. He did all right but the follow-up question was "Where are you from?" He responded, "New York." The DI got in his face and asked, "New York – what?" He responded, "New York City, stupid." Immediately the DI decked him. Everyone seemed to get abused physically or mentally as they went through seventy-four guys. Finally, the seventy-fifth guy was asked, "Where are you from?" He responded, "Florida, you don't like it?" All we heard was fists hitting him with grunts and thuds for at least five minutes. We dared not turn around.

After this exercise in humiliation we proceeded to the barbershop. Every last hair was clipped from our heads. By this time we were all dressed in military issue. Each set of utilities had at least twenty tags on them. We were forbidden to remove any of them. We were told we were not Marines and unworthy to wear the uniforms of brave Marines who paid the supreme sacrifice. They also said that Marines were still suffering from injuries sustained while fighting for us peons.

On we went to the Commissary where were issued personal items. There was shaving lotion, blades, soap, a mandatory purchase of a brush to scrub fingernails, a can of brass polish for belt buckles and various related items. The military was advancing us money and we had the option of buying cigarettes. We hadn't had a butt since we landed in this God forsaken place and I looked forward to a smoke. After the shopping venture, we were told that there would be a regular inspection to insure we didn't smoke. One could only smoke when "the smoking lamp was lit."

We were marched into the dining area, which was referred to as the Mess Hall, for lunch and supper that day. We had to march sideways with our trays in front of us and parallel to the chow line. There was no selecting food. Everyone was given the same portion on a metal tray. It was mandated that we had to eat everything and we did. Finally, towards the end of the day, we were marched to our barracks. They were referred to as "Nissan Huts" and each one accommodated sixteen men. They resembled metal sheds. Johnny Coffey was sent to a different hut, and I wouldn't have the opportunity to talk to him for at least six weeks and that was in the form of a short whisper. We were then assigned a bunk bed. There were double bunks in each hut. After we put down our sea bags, we marched to another location where we got a mattress, sheets and blankets. We also got a pillow and pillowcase. When we returned to the barracks, we were told how to make a bed with hospital corners.

I had been assigned a bottom bunk. The top one was assigned to the guy with the smart mouth from Florida, Private Parker.

We then showered and were told, "Lights out." To be more accurate, there was only one light bulb on the rounded ceiling. There was a heater in the middle of the hut but we were told it is to remain off. No one would be allowed to touch it. There was nothing that could go on fire. Everything was made of metal and concrete. There was one heater, which we weren't allowed to use and no one had a cigarette they dared to smoke.

This was the worst day of my life. I was in a state of fear. The only reason I could sleep was the fact that I was totally exhausted.

The next morning, I was awakened by the DI yelling, "Get out of those racks." He turned on the 100-watt bulb and charged directly at me. I was half asleep but already filled with the fear of God. I was groping for my glasses under the bunk. He grabbed Private Parker out of the top bunk and proceeded to beat him to a pulp. He threw him through one of two doors and walloped him in a manner that I had rarely seen before. As Parker stood dazed, Sergeant Gonzalez said we had twenty minutes to "shit, shower, shave and make our bunks."

We had to run into the cool February air in our skivvies to the bathroom, which is called a "head." It was a scene of chaos. We got beaten for not making our beds properly, having missing tags on our clothes, for not shaving properly and for countless other things. As we fell in ranks, the DI asked, "Who is Private Jackson." A voice responded, "Here, sir!" With that, the DI beat on him. He was told that he went to college with the Company Captain. He alleged that he was probably the Captain's friend and so he beat him some more and said he hated the Captain. Private Jackson's face was all swollen and cut as we lined up for another day in the Corps.

We were not allowed newspapers and we didn't know where we could get one if we wanted to. There were no radios or TVs and we felt cut off from the human race. The second day was a day of learning the rules. We had to memorize the "Positions of Attention," and we were given a booklet containing basics to remember. By now we knew we were dead meat if we didn't remember our Serial Number. This was the day we were given initial instructions on how to march. For the twelve weeks we were at Parris Island, we marched everywhere from early morning to late at night. If we weren't marching, we were duck walking or lining up somewhere toe to heel.

That evening was our first mail call. If you got a letter and it smelled of perfume, you didn't read it but you literally ate it. If you got food, you ate it on the spot while getting punched in the belly until you puked. After mail call, the DI asked if anyone thought they could beat him. Private Billy Boyd said he could kick the DI's ass. I met him on the train. He was a runner up in the heavy weight, "Golden Gloves" at Madison Square Garden. The DI invited him to step out of ranks. He greeted him with a drop kick that knocked Billy out. He proceeded to kick him when he was down.

Two recruits cracked up mentally in those first two days. We were told they were given "Section Eights" (Medical Discharges). They had lost all their confidence and could not perform the simplest of details. We had three guys in our Platoon with the last name of Allen and they all cracked up. It was sad when I observed one of them who got to the point where he couldn't make his own bed.

It was in that first week when a Private Garrett was assigned "fire watch." He was questioned on his "General Orders" and knew them. All of us had to memorize them. He had to patrol all the huts inside and out for four hours during the night. He was so exhausted, he fell asleep standing up and was brought up on a Court Martial. He was found guilty and sentenced to six months in the brig (military jail). This was so unfair and must have had something to do with his being black.

The weeks were spent enduring "chicken shit" (spit and polish), learning protocol, military discipline and paying the price if you made a mistake. We all earned unflattering nicknames. Mine was Private Cokes, referring to the thickness of my lenses.

After three weeks or so, we were assigned to "mess duty." All this time, most guys were constantly hungry but we were restricted in how much we could eat. The "scullery" was my first assignment. In the scullery we had to clean over a thousand meal trays after the troops had eaten. The water temperature was scalding and you weren't allowed protective aprons or gloves. After enduring pain for the first ten minutes in the morning, your hands became numb and you were able to handle the scorching trays as they exited the dishwasher. If a speck of food was found on a single tray, all of them were thrown on the ground and had to be washed a second time -- there were well over a thousand trays. Once, I had to carry a GI can (garbage can) filled with cold cuts to the "Dempsey Dumpster." On the way, when no one was looking (or so I thought) I threw a piece of ham into my mouth. I was immediately tackled by three Sergeants and was told to eat the entire can full of food. I thought this was too good to be true and started to eat. After about twenty minutes of non-stop eating, they whacked me a couple more times and told me to get back to work.

Being wet all day was a problem. One night when I went to take my shower, I observed that my foot was jet black. I refused to say anything, as scary as it seemed because if I did, they'd send me to "sickbay" with the contingent of gay sailors. I'd probably be kept in the infirmary and then reassigned another Platoon destined for mess duty. The next night, my entire leg was black and the following night every part of me that didn't stick out of my uniform was black. When I got off mess duty, the blackness disappeared in one day. I guess it was a fungus that attacked my body. Once I was dry it disappeared.

Several more recruits cracked up mentally and the DIs took joy in it. Sergeant Gonzalez said he was Mexican and hated whites and blacks. At night, he'd beckon me to his hut. I had to hit the metal exterior of his hut with all my strength, only to be told, he couldn't hear me. After several attempts, he finally said, "Git in here!" At this point, I had to take three steps forward and remain as mute as a lamb before the shears. Finally he'd say, "Git me a coke!" He'd give me money and then I had to run about a half mile to the "slop shoot" (non-commissioned officer's bar and grill), which was forbidden turf for recruits. Outside the bar was a Coke machine along with candy machines. I then had to run back to the DI's hut within a certain time. I was always told I was too slow and got a couple belts in the mid section for being tardy. The DI then retreated with his Coke and had his vodka.

An iron was purchased by every four recruits; we used it to press our clothes. Once, Corporal Bailey came into the hut and took the iron as I was using it. He told me to report to his hut later to get it back. When I did, I screwed up. I said, "Sir Private Bailey reporting as ordered." He threw the iron at me and I ducked as it whizzed by. It landed on the bulkhead (wall) and broke into many pieces. I told my fellow recruits I'd buy another if we ever got back to the commissary.

Private Terwilliger couldn't wait for the cigarette lamp to be lit. He was caught in the head one night having an illegal cigarette. He was told to report to the DI whenever Platoon 60's smoking lamp was lit. Fortunately for him, the lamp was rarely lit but he certainly paid the price about four times. That was the total amount of cigarette breaks at Parris Island.

We all had to subscribe to the official Marine Corps Magazine called "The Leatherneck." I don't think anyone ever got a copy. It was an obvious scam and someone ripped us off.

We also had to have our picture taken for the yearbook. We all had to buy that, too. When Private Jackson was photographed, the DI put his barracks cap in front of his face. You couldn't even see who it was in the picture. All the damage inflicted on his face was concealed by his barracks cap.

After a month, we all traveled to the rifle range. There we were assigned different accommodations. We were now in "Quonset Huts," which was a larger version of the "Nissan Hut." We were issued rifles and range jackets. We were also given a booklet describing our weapon (M-1 Rifle) in detail. We had to memorize its serial number and know the windage and elevation setting for 200, 300 and 500 yards. We were told how to take it apart and put it back together. We spent every day drilling with the rifles, cleaning them and dry firing them for a couple weeks. Finally we fired the rifles for a week. Surprisingly, I did well and on qualification day fired "sharpshooter" despite a malfunction with my rifle. I had a near perfect score going back to the 500-yard line. A Colonel approached me and told me I'd better get a bulls-eye or he would kick my ass. I fired off a round but my target didn't come down. He picked up the Double-E Eight (field telephone) and warned the recruit manning the target that he'd better find a hole in the bulls-eye or he'd come down and find one in his head. The target came down and went up again immediately with a marker indicating I hit the middle of the bulls-eye. The Colonial then proceeded to kick me in the ribs. It was impossible to breathe properly and sweat was rolling down my glasses, which hindered my eyesight. This time they followed my next round with binoculars and determined that I had what's referred to as a "stock rub." This had an adverse effect on my score, but the overall score was rated as sharpshooter. Whoever didn't qualify (one or two), were sent back to another Platoon after being scourged at the pillar.

While we were at the rifle range, the Platoon after us (Platoon 61) experienced an incident that captured national attention. Their DI drowned six recruits in the quicksand. We only heard about it in the letters we received from our families and we couldn't discuss the topic. The culprit was Technical Sergeant McKeon. The matter even caused Congress to review the training procedures in this hellhole. We were marching one day and a man in civilian clothes kept calling aloud, "Sergeant, Sergeant!" After a dozen attempts to get Sergeant Gonzalez's attention, the Platoon was brought to a halt. The man asked if he could speak to him for a moment and introduced himself as a U.S. Senator. Sergeant Gonzalez shouted, "I don't see any stripes on your arm." He then gave the command to march, ignoring the Senator.

It was my understanding that Sergeant McKeon was brought up on a military court martial and found guilty. He was sentenced to six months in the brig. Six months later, he received all his stripes back and retired as a Technical Sergeant.

To me, this was so unjust. Private Garrett fell asleep on fire watch while there was no threat of fire and was given the same punishment as this Sergeant who was responsible for the deaths of six men. Prejudice reigned supreme in those days. The one worse thing than being a Private in the Marine Corps was being a black Private in the Corps.

On most days, I managed to stay out of trouble. It was sad seeing so many guys cracking up mentally. One day when I was cleaning my rifle, I dropped a speck of linseed oil on the deck. A Private Hunt was assigned as our "Hut Mother." In his Alabama drawl, he commanded me to clean it up. I said I would. I also told him not to get his bowels in an uproar, which was overheard by the DI. Sergeant Gonzalez proceeded to pounce on me and reminded me that the assigned Hut Mother was in control in his absence, which rarely occurred. He then poured out about a pint of the oil on the deck and demanded that I lick it up. There were a few options that I had but elected to choose the path of least resistance and decided to lick it up. In my heart, I knew my day would come and I looked forward to kicking Private Hunt's ass.

One day, Sergeant Gonzalez caught me moving my head as I reacted to a loud noise. From that point on in training I had to wear my cover sideways on my head to remind me of this grave infraction.

My hunger persisted and I managed to throw a handful of carrots in my utility jacket grenade pocket a few times. Once, we were being punished and ordered to "duck walk." We had to squat down and hold our ankles and march. It was raining and we were plodding through mud as the carrots fell to the ground. Naturally, the DI was standing near me and witnessed the episode. He dipped the carrots in the mud and had me eat them. I actually enjoyed them but gave him no such indication. After that, I didn't care to sneak anything out of the Mess Hall.

There was an obvious prejudice that existed. On Sundays, Catholics were given the opportunity to go to Mass, but if you accepted the offer you knew you'd pay the piper. You were ridiculed and reminded how the time detracted from training. As you fell in after Mass, you were found guilty of taking a wrong move in ranks and beaten.

There was only one Jew in our Platoon, Private Oris. It must have been common knowledge that Jews weren't welcomed in the Corps. At one point in training, we were entering a booby-trapped village. We were told never to enter through the front door. The approved tactical maneuver was to have two men hold a rifle between them, have the selected intruder run, place his foot on the rifle they were holding and allow himself to be propelled to the window on the second floor. Private Oris was selected to demonstrate. The DI said, "Gimme the Jew!" Private Oris ran at full speed towards the rifle and when he extended his leg, the Drill Instructors dropped the rifle. Oris slammed into the side of the building as the shingles broke and fell to the ground. Sergeant Gonzalez said the lesson learned was, "Never drop your rifle." As I recall, Private Oris went to sickbay with his injuries but managed to return to Platoon 60.

It was fortunate for me that I had training on the bars. I could grunt and groan and deliver any number of pull-ups, sit-ups or duck walk marathons. If I ran out of steam, fear and faith in God got me over the hurdles every time.

After all the turmoil in basic training, we had a graduation exercise. We marched to music for the first time and listened as the "Marine Corps Hymn" was played. A feeling of intense pride went through our bodies. We were now considered one of the few, the proud.

Once training at Parris Island was finished, we were sent home on ten days' leave. As we arrived by bus at the Port Authority, Tiny's mother and father welcomed me as I got off the bus. They asked me where their son was. I pointed out that he was next to me. A smile was on his face but he was about one hundred fifty pounds of muscle. He had lost a hundred pounds.

When I arrived home, I didn't know what to expect. My mother, of course, threw her arms around me and my dad shook my hand and said he was proud of me. It was a good feeling, knowing my dad got over his anger towards me. It felt good putting on civilian clothes. My dad said "Son, let me buy you a beer." I said "Okay." Then he said, "Put on your uniform." I did and he was thrilled to introduce me to his friends. Parris Island was still a place of interest in the daily papers. The general public was still talking about the six recruits that were drowned.

My brother, Larry, was proud of me but was, unfortunately, jealous. After being rejected by the Navy because of his Diabetes, he contracted tuberculosis and spent a year in a hospital at Oneonta, New York in preparation for surgery. The operation was a success and he was now working as a stone setter on major structures such as Madison Square Garden and the World Trade Center. While at our favorite drinking spa, he instigated a fight. I was angry with him for being a troublemaker but he dismissed my concerns with a chuckle.

When I returned to Parris Island, I was assigned to a "Casual Company" that was never casual. I was still a peon and was treated accordingly. Afterwards, I went through several weeks of infantry training. Then they sent me to my first assignment. It was First Radio Company. It was there where I learned to be a radio operator and eventually traveled to Japan and many islands in the Pacific. Hawaii was beautiful. This took place a little more than ten years after the war.

While on Okinawa, we went out on daily exercises in the field after breakfast. We were given "C-Rations" for lunch and returned past a village consisting of mud huts to the Mess Hall for dinner. We had accumulated about twelve cases of rations; good for over a hundred meals which were in the back of a deuce and a half truck. This day, I kicked the cases off the truck as we drove through the village. I was a sergeant now and my friends and fellow Marines purposely saw nothing. The next day when we drove through that village, everyone threw us kisses.

This was an incident that helped change my life. I never felt closer to God. The fact that I risked a Court Martial meant nothing.

The country was at peace until one day when we were called to fall in. We were told we were going to war. The Sergeant inquired, "Any questions?" I asked, "With whom are we going to war?" The response was, "None of your business." Later I found out our destination would have been Lebanon. Half my company boarded a plane the next day. After a week, we were once again told to fall in. The announcement was that the war was over. Again, we were asked if anyone had any questions. Naturally, I had to inquire who won.

One of the troops in our outfit was Lebanese and spoke the language. He was sent with the first contingent of troops for obvious reasons. He was used as a linguist for General Wade. After the war was over, he was busted and was reduced in rank to PFC, which he was when he left for Lebanon. He wasn't well liked and wore out his welcome with the brass.

After three years in the Corps, I was honorably discharged. One of my buddies had a car and we drove through the gate at Camp Geiger for the last time.

The MP put up a signal to stop but we gave him the finger and kept going.

4

LOVE AT FIRST SIGHT

For the first time in my life, I realized that time was speeding by and I couldn't say there was a meaningful thing that I accomplished. I was living in my own world. My girlfriend, Helga and I had a relationship that was going nowhere. She dated other guys while I was away but I didn't really care and had no interest in rekindling our fire. As a matter of fact, her lack of loyalty turned me off.

Again, I resorted to prayer. The Marine Corps couldn't crack me up but did knock the senselessness out of me. God had been good to me. He gave me parents who had very little materially, but blessed me with their faith and love. He gave me two wonderful brothers and the skills to survive poverty and oppression. He gave me courage when it was needed and it was needed often.

My life was now entering a new chapter. I wanted it to have real meaning. I seriously thought about becoming a priest but felt unqualified and incompetent. Also, I never wanted to make a career move that was so permanent that I couldn't change my mind. The thought of "once a priest, always a priest" was too scary. I was, however, talking about real conversion; not the Sunday afternoon type that happens every week in an outdoor tent down south for "whites only." I was disgusted with the manner that we were treating our fellow humans in ghetto areas of our cities and in the military of our great United States. Prejudice brought about anger generated between races because of unjust laws and a constitution that brave men died for in vain. There was no real equity among people. Children were the most vulnerable to the oppression that existed. Surely, our forefathers didn't intend our liberty to be tainted with prejudice and bias.

I prayed to the Blessed Mother and asked for the impossible. It was my wish to be ordained and live for Christ and bring his love to others. This was strange for someone who had just spent three years learning how to kill, but I was as sincere then as I am now.

In order to accomplish what I had in mind, I had to start by meeting the right girl and raise the family I always dreamed of. There was no doubt in my mind that this prayer would be heard and answered. This was despite the fact that a married man at that time couldn't be ordained in the Catholic Church.

The GI Bill was discontinued temporarily as far as education was concerned and I needed a job immediately. I had no wheels and the Marine Corps Bank even embezzled me out of $50.00 claiming I had never put the money in. Senator Javits responded favorably to my letter and heads hung. I wasn't the only Private at Parris Island who was scammed. As my father would say, "Bad luck to them!"

At least now I had the military service behind me and employers didn't have that excuse not to give me a job. My immediate thought was to become a cop, but my eyesight wasn't good enough despite the fact that I ran ten miles a day, did 500 sit-ups and about forty chins and pull ups.

On my first weekend out of the military, I went to my cousin, Betty's, wedding in Brooklyn. At a bar before the reception, my Godfather's next door neighbor, Tom Rogers, asked what I was doing with myself. I told him I was going job hunting on Monday. He then said that he would do what he could at his job for me but couldn't promise. I asked him what kind of work he did. He said he worked for Pinkerton's Detective Agency. Immediately, I declined saying I wasn't interested in guard duty but he assured me that it would be investigative work. Based on this promise I figured I'd check it out. I told him I had no experience in this field but he said they'd train me. I went to Broad and Nassau Street that Monday at 9:00 a.m. hoping for a break. As I got off the elevator, the Vice President, Frank Trecose, met me and he arranged to have me fingerprinted and introduced to the Board of Directors (Tom Rogers was the Treasurer). There was a brief orientation and I reported to a large room where the investigators did their paperwork. All of them stared at me. I was the youngest by at least twenty-five years. All of them seemed to be ex-cops with invaluable years of training. Their investigative skills were unsurpassed. In order to get off on the right foot, I stood up and introduced myself, told them I just got out of the Corps and got my job through sheer nepotism. They laughed at my honesty and many later told me they appreciated my truthfulness, shook my hand and offered their help and advice should I want it.

My first paycheck arrived just before the weekend and Dooley and I decided we'd go to "The Tuxedo Ballroom" where we might pick up chicks. The word was that the Yorkville Section of Manhattan was a fun place to go. Irish music was the rage. We arrived at the Tuxedo Ballroom and I sat with Dooley to have a couple of beers. All of a sudden I spotted a young lady dancing and even though it was unlike me, I asked her for a dance. She was beautiful and had the bubbliest personality I had ever witnessed. Her eyes were the prettiest blue and green I had ever seen. She had a great figure and made me feel special just being with her. I was thrilled when she agreed to dance with me. We were on the dance floor through a dozen numbers before they dimmed to lights to announce that one of the greatest evenings in my life had ended. Her name was Maureen Moloney. I asked her if I could take her home and she agreed if her two girlfriends could accompany us. Without hesitation, I agreed. I didn't want this girl to disappear from my life. I'd never forgive myself. We hailed a "checker cab" and she and her two friends, who were neighbors, jumped in. We dropped them off a block from her apartment house at 1090 Amsterdam Avenue. The sixty family building was on the verge of being condemned. It was being managed by the Port Authority of New York. The Moloney family was the sole tenant remaining in this vast apartment complex. Nevertheless, they had an elevator operator around the clock and security as well. Maureen's father, Denis, told the representative from the Port Authority that they would have to find him a place to live at the same or less rent in a decent building nearby because he liked the neighborhood. By the way, he wanted another four-room apartment on the top floor in the rear of an apartment house. The Port Authority threatened all the other families and bullied them into vacating the structure to make room for the Cross Bronx Expressway. This bureaucratic agency was formed to improve commerce for the Port of New York. Instead, they became realtors and art collectors while every ship left our harbor on a one-way trip. The great ships of Moore McCormick, Grace, and the United States Lines are only a memory. The Port Authority is nothing more than glorified toll collectors and an employment agency for politicians to send their constituents; a place where the benefits are great, nepotism flourishes, and pensions are ideal for everyone except the taxpayer. Somehow, the police and emergency workers have managed to stand tall and be counted despite the Port's mismanagement.

Well, Denis Moloney challenged their might and he got his apartment with all his stipulations. Although the rent was higher, the Port Authority subsidized the increase.

When I escorted Maureen to her door that night, I settled for a kiss on the cheek. She agreed to go out with me on a date in the future. She told me that she had been engaged but called it off because her mother-in-law to be was so dominant that her relationship would have never lasted.

On our first date, I took her to the RKO Movie Theatre on 181 Street and Broadway across the street from a Horn and Hardart, where a cup of coffee was still a nickel. She preferred to sit in the balcony. As we sat down, foul-mouthed teenagers were all around us. There must have been ten of them and they were very disrespectful and vulgar. After a couple minutes of listening to them, I said loudly in the voice I used as a Sergeant in the Marines, "Knock it off!" They shut up quickly but one punk turned around and gave us a contemptuous look. With that, Maureen stood up and said, "Come on, we'll take you all on!" I couldn't believe my ears. Her voice rang out with conviction and the whole lot of them decided to be quiet and watch the movie or face the rage of a young woman without fear.

On another date, I found out that she was once attacked in the subway by a molester; she had carried a can opener with her and slashed the perk's face. She then accompanied him to police headquarters where he was to be charged. The guy's pregnant wife showed up and Maureen gave it up when her tears started flowing. Hopefully, he never attacked another young woman. My guess is that he was afraid he'd meet up with another can opener. Bad luck to him!

My job at Pinkerton was going well but I worked the weirdest hours. I'd always fall asleep on the subway. Once, I woke up on the IRT Subway and someone took a razor and cut my wallet out of my trousers. I felt the draft and I think that's what woke me up.

Another time, I fell asleep and went past my stop in the wee hours of the morning. I woke up at Rector Street and this guy was removing the wallet from my pocket. I went to grab it and it fell to the ground. He managed to get out while the doors were closing on him. I got my wallet and sprung after him. I also managed to wrestle with the doors as well and also exited the subway car. I proceeded to chase him up the several flights of stairs and caught him on the very top step. I lifted him up by the heels and banged his head on every step all the way back to the subway platform. Then I took his money. I wanted him to know what it felt like to be pick-pocketed. I wanted this maggot to be the victim for a change. Bad luck to him!

Afterwards, I felt guilty for what I did. Certainly, my actions were no better than his. My decision to put the money in the poor box at Saint Francis Church on 33rd Street was a good one.

My brother, Larry, loved to instigate fights. In the "Full Moon," our favorite bar and grill, we had many a fight. One night there were sailors at the end of the bar and after a few beers, Larry said his brother was a Marine and could kick their asses. Naturally, they were high and a fight broke out. I had no desire to fight but there were no other options on the table. I found solace in the fact that Larry ended out with a shiner.

My dates with Maureen were frequent. She heard that I frequented the "Full Moon" and said that it was she or the bar; she didn't want to date a person that drank. By this time, I was madly in love with her and nothing else seemed to matter in my life. My choice was her and I was pleased to have such an option. By now, I had warmed up to her mom and dad and I introduced her to my parents. They loved her and recalled what I had said years before, "The girl I bring home is the girl I'll marry." It was humorous when she asked to go to the bathroom in my old apartment. She came out and whispered that she couldn't find the handle to flush the toilet. I was somewhat embarrassed to tell her the toilet was flushed by pulling a chain on an overhead tank. My apartment, although neat and well kept, was never featured in Better Homes and Gardens.

Her mother, Bea, and I got along extremely well. I rarely saw her father because he worked evenings. He treated me with respect but told me he looked forward to a son-in-law who could lift heavy weights and have a nice car. Needless to say, I fell short in both categories.

One evening, I was at Maureen's apartment watching television. Her mother was in the kitchen. As I lit up a cigarette, a spark went behind the couch. There were no signs of fire so I put my arm back around Maureen and continued to watch the show. In no time, a blazing fire heated my arm. I ran to the kitchen and got pots of water and threw them on the flames and the fire was finally doused. Needless to say, this was one of the most embarrassing nights of my life. There was a hole two foot square in the back of the couch. Maureen's mom told me not to worry. I offered to pay for a new one but she declined. It happened that Bea Moloney reported the fire to her insurance company and got a much better couch with the money. Maureen was also very forgiving.

In those days, my brother, Frank, was in the Army and stationed in Hawaii.

Something came up and I had to go downtown, New York. As I got on the subway I realized that I forgot my wallet. Also, I neglected to give my dad a message and all I had was a dime in my pocket. After thinking it through, it dawned on me that I could use the dime to call my dad collect. The operator would give me back the ten cents and I'd have enough for the return subway trip. So I called my dad collect. When he answered, "Who is this?" I answered, "It's your son." He said, "Son, don't worry about the charges," thinking it was Frank in Hawaii. I was taken back with his Irish brogue. I never realized he had an accent until I heard him on the phone. Finally, I persisted, "Dad, it's Joe." He retorted, "Bad luck to you son!" and he hung up on me. Needless to say, he was peeved when I got home. He insisted that I should have given him the message.

After my brother finished his tour of duty in Hawaii, he was relocated to Fort Chaffee, Arkansas. One weekend, he drove to Kansas City, Kansas to visit our Aunt Catherine. This was a very interesting visit because Catherine had immigrated to the United States at the age of twelve, on the very same day that my mother was born. Naturally, when my mom arrived in this country, she wanted to locate her sister. She wrote a letter to the Department of War in Washington, DC. and received an answer only a few days later in the pre-computer age. She had said that her sister was a nurse in World War I. They included my aunt's married name and address in the letter. Neither my mom nor Catherine had the money for travel, so they stayed in touch by writing. However, after my brother visited my aunt, they called each other once a month but never met. Finally the day came, when my aunt died and my mom and her sister, Liz, flew out with Frank and arranged her burial.

Among Aunt Catherine's belongings were books, with the same titles as the ones my mother collected over the years. They never discussed the works of literature they cherished but they obviously were much alike.

This was certainly a different era. The first thing my mother saw in the United States was the Statue of Liberty. I had asked her how she felt when she saw it. She said that she cried and I asked her why. She said she felt unworthy to be in this great country.

After I got out of the service, my parents bought their first home. My father was always reluctant to own a house and tried to no avail to convince my mother. She was determined. My dad agreed to look for a house for her but had no intentions of buying one. When she found a nice house in the Kingsbridge Section of the Bronx, he refused to see it because it was made of wood. She found a brick house but he said it didn't have a slate roof. Then she found a house made of Belgium Brick with a slate roof. He looked at that one but the owner wanted $21,000 and he offered $17,000. I'm sure he felt his offer would be unacceptable but the estate was anxious to sell and offered it for $18.000. My father refused but for some unknown reason the house was sold to my parents for $17,000. Many years later, I found out that my mother paid $1,000 under the table to close the deal.

My father jumped at the opportunity for cheap labor. He showed me how to remedy a leakage problem in the house and braced me for the preventive solution. He had me dig a ditch the length of the house. He had me save all the rocks and he tarred the outside wall to stop all water from finding its way into the basement in the future. He knew what he was doing. The extra soil from the dig created a garden for my mom. This was probably the greatest gift I could have given her. She had every kind of plant and tree growing in her Garden of Eden. One of her plants she referred to as a wild carnation. While it was in bloom, I'd pluck a flower from the plant and brought it with me as I commuted to work. I'd meet Maureen on the 168th Street platform of the IND Subway and give her the flower and a peck on the cheek each morning while the straphangers cheered. They'd position themselves for the best view of our early morning rendezvous.

The Moloney Family invited me to their weekend home in Port Jefferson, Long Island. Maureen and I were to meet them there. We were to take the Long Island Railroad. Maureen and I met as planned. She was wearing a large straw hat with a blue ribbon on it. She never looked more beautiful. She had a white dress with blue flowers. She caught the glances of everyone as she walked by them. We selected the last car of the train from Jamaica. She was describing the house as my eyes were glued to her beautiful smile and vibrant look on her face that was exclusively hers. The train stopped at one of the Island's usual stations and the conductor got off to buy cigarettes. The next thing we knew, the conductor was running after the train shouting, "Pull the cord!" Maureen responded more quickly than I. She started pulling the emergency cord but it was obvious that it wasn't connected to anything. Nevertheless, she yanked the cord like a longshoreman and there must have been five hundred feet on the floor when she finally came to the realization that pulling the cord did no one any good. Meanwhile, I was hysterical laughing. At first, she failed to see the humor in it but finally joined in the laughter with many others. Passengers had verbally transmitted the SOS and the engineer stopped the train for the conductor to hop aboard.

It was amazing that Mr. Moloney managed to build this house on his own and did so by reading a book that was entitled, "How to Build a House for Under $5,000." Unfortunately, he also listened too attentively to neighbors who lived in the area for many years. One old man, a Mr. Wynn Darling, encouraged him to build it close to the road because the cost of a water pipe now exceeded a dollar a foot. The whole construction was riddled with problems and as the years progressed, I became the one to fix them. There was never time for recreation at this confounded spot where no one would ever give anyone else the right of way. I sensed all the neighbors knew Denis Moloney's short temper. I felt like a Yankee living down South. I hated the town and laughed because there was a twenty-year wait for a boat slip. Millionaires frequented the Port Jefferson Harbor. They enjoyed the amenities of the upper class while tourists swarmed the inexpensive eateries near the pier for fast food. It seemed all of the residents were unfriendly; but then again, could the problem have been my father-in-law, who was ill tempered and ill-mannered while at the same time being angry at the world. He hated our country and felt we never did anything for him. He told me how he came to our shores with an education and paid his taxes.

Many times, I suggested he go back to Ireland but he just shrugged me off. I think he had more enemies there than here. However, I loved his daughter and she loved him. I didn't want anything negative to interfere with our relationship.

We were dating for less than a year when I asked her for her hand in marriage. I popped the question at Midnight Mass at Incarnation Church in Washington Heights on Christmas Eve in 1959. She said, "Yes" and I was thrilled.

One of her greatest supporters was my Aunt Nonie. She had come to live with my mom and dad when her eyes failed her. She had cataracts and didn't do as instructed by her doctor. The end result was that she had to give up her apartment and moved in with us. When I announced my engagement to Maureen, she acted like a young schoolgirl and said that she had a special present for Maureen. She dispatched my brothers Larry and Frank, who was recently discharged from the Army, to bring out the cedar chest she brought with her from Ireland at the turn of the century. She told Maureen that this was now her hope chest as it was at one time hers. Inside was a woolen blanket wrapped up with a large Kelly green bow. She explained that the blanket was made for her when she was a small girl in Ireland on the family's sheep farm. It kept her warm for many years. She then opened the blanket and everyone's face dropped. There must have been a hundred moth holes in it. No one dared to laugh. Instead, tears rolled down our cheeks. There was never a greater act of love exhibited in the Niland Family. My aunt was the only member of my grandparent's generation that I ever met. She was my godmother and someone I cherished knowing. It was difficult for me to comprehend that the blanket was weaved by my great grandmother with the wool sheared from the sheep by my great grandfather.

No matter what time I'd come home, my Aunt Nonie would be waiting for me. I'd always have a cup of tea with her and read her, "Dear Abbey," which appeared in the Daily Mirror. I'd verbally change the letters Abby received and my aunt would question me. Once I called her bluff, I'd hold the paper in front of her and say, "I told you." Rather than admit she couldn't see, she conceded and believed everything I said. We shared many great laughs and memories together. She was one of the saints I encountered in my life and she had a positive influence on me. I sensed that she prayed a great deal for me and God knows I needed it.

Maureen and I were beginning to have serious discussions about our future together. We both had the same ideals, which weren't complicated. We wanted someday to own our own home, have children and make a difference in the world.

Things were going great for me at Pinkerton's, but was it my connections? Maureen and I decided that our future plans could not work if I continued to work at Pinkerton's because it was national. If I got promoted, it would mean being transferred to another city. It was at that time I sought employment elsewhere and ended up working at the Automobile Club of New York. The benefits were terrific and employment had a history of being steady during difficult times.

It was humorous when I went to my job interview. The representative from the Auto Club's name was Mr. Newland. When I arrived, he greeted me. "Good morning, I'm Mr. Newland and your name is?" I responded "Joe Niland." He said, "No, Newland, not Niland." I responded, "No, my name is Niland." He then said, "I see." Isn't it strange we have the same name? Right then, I figured I'd never get this job. However, we finally got the names right and I was hired.

That night, Maureen and I celebrated by going out to a simple dinner. This was something we hadn't been doing. We were saving our money. As the evening came to a conclusion, I walked her home. As we were about to part company, I went to kiss her. Kidding around, she pulled away and a bobby pin stuck me in the nose. Blood gushed out but I put my head back and the bleeding stopped.

The next day, I was in a training class at the Auto Club. While marking a trip-tik map, blood poured from my nose. In order to stop the bleeding, I put my head back and put my feet on the desk. At that moment, the Director walked in. Naturally, his first impression of me was not a good one. In the panic mode, I sat upright. Immediately, he understood why I had resorted to the restful position I had assumed as the blood poured once again.

That evening, I told Maureen what had happened and we had a good laugh. However, during my spell of laughter, my nose started bleeding again. This time it couldn't be stopped. It was necessary for me to go to the hospital emergency. There was no, "HIPAA Law" a law which prohibits discussing any patient's medical condition without the patient's approval and the doctors and nurses enjoyed a good laugh when I told them the wound was inflicted on me when I attempted to kiss my fiancé good night.

Those early days at Triple A provided me with plenty of overtime. My finances were reduced to zero when I bought Maureen's engagement ring for $460.00. It was now time to save for an apartment and furniture. Naturally, we decided to find a cheap apartment so we could save for a house. We set our wedding date for February because June weddings were through the roof as far as expenses were concerned.

We found our first apartment in the Bronx on Bailey Avenue. It was a six-story walk up. The place was like a disaster area. It took two months to sand the floors, spackle, paint, and replace the kitchen sink. The rent was $65.00 a month. We bought good furniture that was somewhat oversized but ideal for a first house. I made all of the repairs, despite the nagging of my father-in-law who laughed at my attempts to fix things. Since I never had similar responsibilities I was ill equipped to handle some of the problems I encountered. Once I was given some sound advice from him, I met the challenge. The apartment was loaded with roaches and every night I left, newspapers were strewn under the door that was emulsified in roach spray. It didn't bother me at first because of the condition of the place but as I developed a pride for my accomplishments it ticked me off. As I would leave the apartment after working at Triple A all day and the apartment in the evening, I'd kick the papers and warn aloud whoever was responsible for such an action. During the time I was working on the apartment, I met all my neighbors to be. One Sunday morning after church, I brought Maureen up to the apartment. She hadn't seen it since I made all the renovations. I introduced her to the neighbors. Mrs. Goode was the lady next door. She told Maureen she had a lovely fiancé but her painter was a terrible person. She had no idea that we were one and the same. I invited her in to see the clean up job and she no longer put papers under the door.

My other neighbors were nice people. The Moran's were a middle-aged couple. Unfortunately, the mother had terminal cancer. They had three beautiful children. The husband was also sick. It was unclear what was wrong with him. Then there was the Bonelli Family. Mr. Bonelli was a comic. When he heard I had been in the Marine Corps, he told me that both of his sons were also in the Corps. I was given a tour of his wall of honor. There were hundreds of pictures of his sons when they were in the service of their country. The FBI now employed them. There was also the Moran's aunt and uncle. They lived opposite our apartment and had a smaller place. In the neighboring building, one of Maureen's girlhood friends, Sandy, lived with her husband, Tommy. We had every intention of getting to know them better in due time.

All the usual plans were made for our wedding; the women's dresses, the tuxedo rentals, the wedding hall, the dinner menu and the tiered cake. Maureen's first cousin, Father Frank Boyle, would witness our vows and the wedding would take place at Incarnation Church, which was the parish that Maureen attended throughout her life. Plans were made to insure that nothing would go wrong. Financially, we figured things out. We didn't have enough for the wedding but we anticipated that the gifts of money would pay the outstanding bills.

5

WEDDING BELLS

We picked February 4, 1961 as our wedding day. Things were much cheaper off-season and we had no choice but to save money. The night before the wedding was one to remember. There was a seventeen-inch snowstorm. My friend, Bob Tomchak, from the Marine Corps came to my parent's house with intentions of staying over. However, when they arrived, his wife, Lucille went into labor and they headed for their hospital in Wilkes-Barre, Pennsylvania. The scotch bottle was opened and Dooley and my brothers joined in with my Dad in sharing memories.

The phone rang frequently. It was usually Maureen who was in the panic mode because her gown would be destroyed in the snow. All the other calls were from friends saying they would do their best to make it to the wedding.

At an ungodly time of the morning, I woke up. The first thing I had in mind was the amount of snow accumulation. I opened the rear door to check and couldn't see daylight. The snow had drifted so high that there was no longer an exit at the rear of the house. A formal check of weather on the TV verified that we had seventeen inches of snow. My father, recovering from the night before, started to get dressed but couldn't find his shoes. Naturally, he asked my mother. She apologized and said she forgot that she had taken them to the shoemaker. He said that he would go get them but she retorted that he would only give them to her. Tony was an old-fashioned Italian shoemaker who did quality work while listening to opera. He gave no tickets to customers. He knew them all by name, which he mispronounced in his Italian accent. My father said, "Don't worry, he'll give me the shoes." Well, Tony told him to get out of his shop when dad demanded shoes that he thought were his. In defiance, my dad took the shoes and left in the snowstorm with Tony yelling at him. When he got home, he discovered that the shoes didn't fit. He said to my mom, "Molly, I got the wrong shoes, could you bring them back." It took a while but she did. When she returned with the shoes, Tony said my father was a mad man and he gave my mom the correct pair of shoes.

Maureen called to tell me that the florist called. They couldn't make it to the church. The limousines were also a cancellation. The worst call came from Father Frank Boyle. He was to be the church's witness to the marriage. He didn't think he could make it but would try. He couldn't drive and all the buses in Riverdale stopped running. He eventually used a garbage can cover and came down about ten flights of steps to Kingsbridge and then took the subway.

Maureen called again. This time she said she was trying to work out something with the Department of Sanitation for transportation to the church.

Eventually, I put on the rented tuxedo and wore my spit-shined "boon dockers" that I had from the Marine Corps and took the subway. Surprisingly, it was running. My brother, Larry was with me. He was the best man. When we entered the room off the Sacristy at Incarnation Church, we were astonished that no one else was in the church. At that time, Larry started to feel ill and collapsed. All the color drained from his face. I knew it was his Diabetes. I ran over to the rectory but no one answered the rear door. I had no other option but to break the glass, which I did. I charged to the refrigerator and grabbed a container of orange juice. I rushed back to the deserted church, where I managed to get some of the juice down Larry's throat. The color came back to his face and he was back to normal within a few minutes.

Again, I looked out in the church and observed that no one including my parents came to my wedding.

However, I later determined that the Sanitation Commissioner, Mr. Scravane, sent six garbage trucks and transported Maureen and her bridesmaids to the church. When Maureen proceeded down the aisle, a Schaefer Beer Can fell from the hoop in her skirt. Maureen's picture was on the front page of the "Journal American" the next day. The headline was, "Love laughs at Blizzard." The featured picture showed the garbage man lifting her from the truck.

Father Frank showed up at the last minute and the ceremony went off pretty well despite the fact that the elaborate aura was sacrificed for the basic rite. All the immediate family made it, along with many friends and neighborhood people who satisfied their curiosity.

After the wedding, we faced the dilemma of getting to the Trocadero Ballroom on Dyckman Street. My brother lay down on Broadway and a Bond bread truck stopped to avoid hitting him. At that point half of the bridal party jumped into the delivery van. The driver was a real sport and dropped us off at the front door of our destination.

The wedding reception was one to remember. Every guest had their own story to tell describing how they got to the reception and everyone claimed there was more snow where they lived. Many people had casual attire or should I say winter survival apparel.

After the wedding, the family returned to my parents' house. After sharing stories, laughs and a few drinks, Maureen and I decided to head for our honeymoon apartment. We had no idea how we'd get to Pennsylvania's, Mount Airy Lodge. We had many gifts to carry back to our new home and my cousin, Tommy Spellman, helped tote the packages several blocks and up the six flights of stairs. When we got to the apartment, I offered Tom a drink and he accepted. However, he was in a talkative mood and showed no intentions of leaving. After all, this was our wedding night. Finally, he took the hints we gave him and we spent our first night together as man and wife.

The next morning, we loaded up my brother, Larry's, Mercury. He gave me a long list of things to be aware of and in a threatening manner told me to take good care of it. Naturally, I complied with his every request. Otherwise, I'd have no car.

The Port Authority Police stopped us at the George Washington Bridge. They were not permitting unnecessary travel. However, when we told them we had reservations at Mount Airy and we were on our honeymoon, they gave us the okay and off we went.

While we were still in Northern New Jersey, Maureen asked if she could drive. Naturally, I reminded her that she had no license. She said, "Don't tell me our marriage is going to be like this." She said she only wanted to drive for a short distance and didn't think I'd make such a big deal of it. I told her that the driving was hazardous. The roads were extremely slippery.

To make matters worse, there were many icy spots; not to mention the fact that we were in my brother, Larry's, car. Despite making a lot of sense, I folded like a cheap camera and paid the price so many guys pay for love. I pulled over and let her get behind the wheel. I then provided her with a litany similar to the one my brother gave to me about his prized Mercury. The car had automatic shift so I didn't have to give clutch instructions. She had no license but possessed a heavy foot. She was driving no more than five minutes when she had to slam on the brakes to avoid hitting another car. The car swerved and went off the road. We skidded down a park-like path and came to rest a couple feet before a cliff, which was the gateway to eternity. Before we stopped, I saw my life flash by. We were in such a precarious position, I opened her door softly and had her exit; and then I eased out the driver's door. I was concerned that the car would slide forward. After many deep breaths and after sizing up my predicament, I got behind the wheel and managed to get back on the road. When we were safe again, I asked myself out loud, "What was I thinking?" She said, "Don't make such a big deal out of it," and she swore me to secrecy. I had no intentions of telling anyone because I didn't want Larry to find out that I let her drive.

We arrived in one piece at Mount Airy and enjoyed lunch. They announced that they had skiing nearby. Maureen said, "Let's go." I told her I never skied before. She laughed and said there is nothing to it. Off we went and rented ski equipment. Then we went to the top of the slope on a tow bar. As I was about to descend, I asked for some instructions? Maureen said to look at the others and I'd get the idea. As I was coming down the slope, I noticed that I didn't have any ski-poles and I had no idea how to stop. However, this was no problem because I crashed into a small brick building at the bottom of the hill. Despite being stunned, I managed to look for Maureen. I was anxious to see her style. Then I saw her, coming down on the tow bar. I asked her why she didn't ski down and she said she never skied before and didn't want to crash as I did.

At that time, a young newlywed fell on the ski slope and was in pain. Her husband rushed to her side. She must have broken her ankle. Maureen showed her compassion and volunteered both of us to accompany them to the nearest hospital. We had the patient sit in the back of their car. Her husband drove and Maureen and I got into the front bench seat. We were moving along at a good pace as the patient's husband navigated the hills of the Pocono Mountains. We took a blind turn and directly in front of us was a car stopped on the highway in Bartonsville. We crashed into the car. I was thrown through the windshield and landed on the car we hit. Surprisingly, I wasn't hurt. However, our car was in flames. I rushed to Maureen's aid. When I looked in the car, there was blood on the back of her sweater and she was slumped over with her head on the dashboard. I straightened her up and got the scare of my life. There was also blood on the front of her sweater. Initially, I thought the gear stick, which was located on the Chrysler's dashboard, went through her chest but that was not the case; her head was bleeding profusely. Her face had struck the rear view mirror and tiny particles of glass were embedded in her forehead. A Good Samaritan provided a blanket on which we put her. With help, the young woman was removed, this time with a broken leg. Her husband had been dazed but was coming around. Maureen was groggy as an ambulance arrived simultaneously with a priest from a parish called Our Lady of the Snows. They decided to transport Maureen first. In the ambulance, the priest held her hand. He provided a comforting little homily while doing so. He assured her that this would probably be the greatest obstacle in her marriage and everything with God's help would be all right from now on. No sooner had those words left his lips than the ambulance skidded and turned over on its side. Everything was in shambles. Finally, another ambulance arrived and took us to the emergency room of the local hospital. No further injuries were inflicted on us from the second crash.

As we entered the hospital, a doctor was on his way out. He saw Maureen and asked me what happened. He volunteered to help. He was a plastic surgeon. Many a prayer did I say for that doctor. Eventually, Maureen was diagnosed with a concussion and since there was no room in the hospital, I was told to have someone available at her bedside and seek medical help if she had any problems related to her injury.

All that week, Maureen was confined to bed. Her face was so badly swollen; you'd hardly recognize her. She called her parents and lied to her father. She said we had a crash and had one stitch on her face. Her father asked to speak to me. He cursed and threatened me. He said nothing ever happened to her when she was in his care and now after one day of marriage she was injured. Little did he know that she had well over a hundred stitches! I was all for telling him the truth but Maureen caught me by surprise when she fibbed.

We also called my folks. My mom cried with the news but I assured her that we'd be okay.

During the week of the honeymoon, Maureen spent almost the full day in bed. Meals were delivered to our suite. I only left her to buy mementos at the gift shop for our parents. I bought her a stuffed skunk, which she enjoyed. It greeted her as a surprise when she woke up from one of her naps.

After the week was over, my nerves were a wreck. I slept no more than a couple hours each night. Now, I had to brace myself for the ride home. Maureen failed to see the humor in offering to let her drive. The trip was no more than a hundred miles but seemed like a thousand. Finally, we came to our first stop, her parent's apartment. Her father would have killed me were it not for the shock when he saw how seriously she was hurt. We recounted for them what had transpired and headed for my parent's house. Upon our arrival, my mother was at the first floor window. She said to use the front entrance. The side and back were treacherous with ice. We went up the front steps. My mom cried when she saw Maureen. Larry was surprised to see that his car was in perfect shape. We failed to mention that the accident took place in a different car. He obviously had mixed emotions. He was pleased we were alive but ecstatic to have his car back in one piece. We were sitting in the living room answering all the inquiries when Maureen reminded me that we left the souvenirs in the car. Immediately, I responded and went out the side door. The ice greeted me and I did a full gainer and landed on my head. My brothers helped me to my feet. I returned to the living room and assured everyone that I'd be okay. I lit up a cigarette to calm my nerves and accidentally set my tie on fire. I scooted to the bathroom and grabbed a glass of water. Immediately, I extinguished the fire but broke the glass and cut my hand.

Finally, we returned to our apartment. I had never been so tired in my life.

Standing in front of our king-sized bed (two twins with a common headboard) I proclaimed my thanks to God for bringing us home alive. I plopped down on the bed in utter exhaustion. In doing so, the two twin beds separated and I fell to the floor, gashing my head on the metal frame. It was necessary for me to go to the emergency room at Columbia Presbyterian Hospital.

The next morning, I figured I'd prepare tea and toast for Maureen. When I turned on the gas, nothing happened. It seems Con Edison never turned on our gas. I knocked on a neighbor's door. The gentleman introduced himself as John and said he'd make tea. He knocked on the door a short time later. He had prepared a wonderful breakfast for the two of us. He responded positively to my invite. He was curious to see the renovations in the apartment and was anxious to meet Maureen. She was lying in bed but fully clad in a robe. When he saw her bruises, he dropped the tray on her. We explained what happened and he gave us raves for the work on the apartment. His place was two and a half rooms. He had put in for our apartment but the under the table money we gave to the super set things for us. He was unwilling to pay up!

On my way back from the local grocery store, I met Andy Bonelli. He started our conversation by asking if I was prejudiced. I told him no. He said, "Good." He was expecting five brothers from Italy and asked how many I could put up for a few nights? Naturally, I didn't know what to make of him. Finally, he told me that he was just kidding. He introduced me to his wife and to several other neighbors. He told me his wife was a drunkard, but later I found out that she never had a drink in her life.

It was fun having close friends to our new home. We were only in our apartment for a couple months when we were told we were going to get new plumbing; and so we did. Holes were made in our kitchen and bathroom floors and pipes were lowered from the roof. Mr. Doyle was on the toilet one day and was startled to see a water bug going across his bathroom floor tiles. He thought he was seeing things but he swore there was writing on the bug's back. He caught it and inspected it closely. The note read, "Love from Andy." There was nothing he wouldn't do for a joke. He drove buses for a living and he'd occasionally get into trouble by going down side streets to drop off old ladies in front of their houses in inclement weather. At one time, he was voted, "Bus Driver of the Year." His picture appeared on the advertising near the commuter straps on all the city buses. When my father-in-law met him, he recognized him as an old acquaintance. He had worked with him at the Railway Express. One day, they were shipping caskets. Andy got in one. When a co-worker opened the box, Andy popped up and almost gave him a heart attack. He was fired.

My brother, Frank, and his wife, Susie, appeared on our doorstep one day. Frank got thrown out of the house and they had nowhere to live. They stayed with us for a couple months until they got their own place. I remember getting up in a crowded apartment with one bathroom. Maureen was up first. She cleaned the house and got breakfast for everyone. I'd get up and get dressed. We'd all have breakfast and then go to work. That is, except Susie. She didn't work. When we got home, the house would be a mess. She did nothing but we hung in there for my brother's sake. Boy, were we happy when they found their own place to live.

Sandy and Tommy Morrissey got the word that they were going to have a baby. We were thrilled for them and we had dreams that we would encounter the same experience. We loved children. Tommy was not very handy and Sandy requested that I check the lock on their front door. There had been a rash of thefts in the apartment house where we lived. When I was going to check out their lock, I brought a screwdriver with me; I rang their bell and nonchalantly tapped the lock as it fell inside on the floor. Sandy saw it was me and realized what had happened and was so thankful when I screwed the lock together properly.

Tommy had gone out and purchased a crib. It took him eight hours to put it together. Finally, he realized that it was too wide to get into the bedroom. He had to take it apart and reassemble it again.

About a month later, Maureen found out that she was pregnant. We were so excited and immediately we started to make plans. I nagged her to take the medicines her doctor prescribed. She refused to listen and insisted that a good diet and exercise was all that was necessary. Many babies at this time were born without limbs due to a medicine called thalidomide. It was a drug prescribed for morning sickness. I thanked God that she ignored her doctor.

One night, Maureen and I were out late and when we got home, we looked up from the courtyard and saw the lights were on in our apartment. We knew we had turned them off. I charged up the steps and saw wet footmarks outside the door. As I entered the apartment, I observed that our furniture was in disarray and all the drawers were emptied on the floor. The television was gone along with our stereo. We felt so violated.

The robbery made me bitter. I went out and got a double barrel shotgun with two shells. I didn't want to entertain the thought that it would be in the apartment and future perpetrators would have the drop on me as Maureen and I entered the apartment. Therefore, I drilled two holes in a closet, inserted the shells and put a thin coat of plaster over the holes. If I wanted to retract the shells, it took a couple ounces of pressure by my fingers and they would slide out into my hand. I was ready for the next invasion.

Several times over the next month, Maureen heard noises and called the police. They were convinced she was hearing things and it was all due to the robbery we incurred.

One night, I came home from work early. I had been working a lot of overtime because we wanted that first house and now with a baby coming, it was more of a priority. I turned off the lights as I lay on the couch. Maureen woke me about an hour later by whispering in my ear. She said there were two men on the fire escape, which was their method of operation. They had broken the window and jimmied the lock when they gained entry to the apartment when we were robbed. I went to the closet, got the shotgun, loaded the weapon and told Maureen to call the cops. I went up on the roof and quietly awaited the arrival of the two thugs. Maureen called the police; they heard the sirens and took off for the rooftop. As the first creep got off the fire escape, I shoved the barrel of the weapon into his mouth taking many teeth with force. Blood gushed down the shotgun as the other thief froze in his tracks. I suggested they listen as I took off the safety with a threatening click. The second man sat where I told him to, with his ass barely on the ledge of the roof. Finally the cops made their appearance and took both of them away.

One of the men lived in the adjacent building. They claimed they were putting up a TV antenna. The word got out that they were druggies and one of them had a brother who was a cop. Naturally, he was out in an hour. It makes you wonder. How many felons are released because they have a relative in police enforcement? I saw him several times and grabbed him by the neck and encouraged him to move elsewhere and he did. His wife stayed behind with their baby. He wasn't much of a husband and wasn't a provider for his family. He was only interested in feeding his drug habit.

Finally, the big day came. We went to Flower Fifth Avenue Hospital where our highly recommended doctor practiced. Maureen was in labor for seventeen hours. Her doctor left several times during the evening, each time he returned to the hospital. He had been drinking. At one point, I grabbed him by the neck, told him to sober up and warned him that I'd break his neck if Maureen or the baby had problems. It was around midnight when a doctor appeared in the waiting room, removed his mask and inquired; "Is Mr. Niland here?" I sat with my in-laws in suspense. Was Maureen all right, was my wonderful baby born; is everything okay? Finally he spoke and said that my wife wanted to remind me that the buses stop running at midnight. I instructed him to tell her we'd be there until the baby was born. He departed and went to assist her. The baby was due shortly.

It was about an hour later when the doctor appeared once again. This time he said I was the father of a healthy son. He weighed eight pounds and was twenty-one inches long. He said I'd be able to see my wife soon but she will be slightly incoherent because of the anesthetic. I was anxious to share my joy with her but for now I wanted to see my son, a miracle from God. At first, I was very concerned when I saw the incubator he was in but the nurse immediately assured me that this was standard operating procedure. His eyes were pristine blue, he was bald, his knuckles were inverted and he was perfect in every way. I knew that Maureen would be extremely happy. She wanted a boy. I prayed for a healthy baby but she prayed for a boy. She wanted a son to carry on the family name and someday, God willing, have a child of his own. Human nature is something, here I'm handed a miracle from God and already I'm thinking of another.

A short time later, Maureen was brought out on a gurney. She was sitting up yelling, "I told you I'd have a boy, I told you we'd have our Denis." I was so excited, and there was a cleaning lady pushing a laundry cart; I pushed her into it and rolled her down the corridor with glee as I sang Danny Boy in celebration of one of the greatest days of my life.

The Moloneys were equally thrilled but were somewhat disappointed that the baby wasn't a girl. We then took a cab to their home and then I proceeded to my apartment.

As I entered the building, I noticed that there were streamers and balloons on the first floor. However, everything was rather orderly. It couldn't have been the remnants of a party; but then again, maybe someone was preparing to have a blast. It was three o'clock in the morning. As I walked to the second floor, I noticed the same theme; and so it was, all the way to the sixth floor. I had no idea what was going on. Finally, as I arrived at my apartment door, I saw a bottle of scotch taped to the door with a message, "Congratulations, Pop." Andy Bonelli had done it again.

6

OUR FIRST HOUSE

U p until the robbery, we enjoyed life to its fullest in that small apartment.

Afterwards, Maureen felt nervous when she was alone with our baby, Denis. However, she wouldn't admit it. For the first time in our lives we felt violated. Our laws should have stricter penalties to deter such crimes. There are few things in life that are more important than the sanctity of one's home.

My in-laws and my parents always grumbled about the six flights of steps they had to climb. However, they were invited every weekend for dinner and despite their grumbling made the trek. My dad had emphysema from being a smoker and working in subway tunnels for over forty years, and I felt concern for him.

One day after a year and a half in that apartment, Maureen surprised me with a phone call at work. She said she would meet me at the subway stop at West 238th Street. She had a surprise! When I came down the subway steps, she was waiting for me. Denis was in his carriage. She took out half a page of stationery paper with scribbling on it. As I held it in my hand, I observed that it was a receipt for payment on a house. The total price was $21,500.00. My emotions were mixed. I was pleased that she took on this initiative but felt I should have been involved in the decision. Nevertheless, I went to talk to the owner, Mrs. McArdle, who showed me the house with tears in her eyes. She had raised a large family there, her husband had passed away and she was going to live with one of her children. The house was well maintained and was located on Tibbett Avenue, only one block from my mother. We bought that house and began to make plans to move in.

After the closing on the property, I rented a truck and made arrangements for the utilities to read meters both in the apartment and the house. My neighbor, John, had planned to move into my apartment and said he'd give me a hundred dollars for the sink I had installed. He didn't want me to tell Mr. Lazarus, the landlord. At the last minute, he told me he changed his mind. I never thought he'd be so deceiving, but he had every intention of moving in. He figured he'd get the sink for nothing. It was too late to make alternate arrangements so I called the landlord, Mr. Lazarus. He wished us luck and gave us a hundred dollars for the sink. He raised the rent for John because of the new sink and John ended out paying more than he had planned. Being a schemer foiled him. It made me feel good that he didn't put one over on us. Bad luck to him!

It was a marvelous feeling--owning our own house. I had painted the entire place before we made the big move. Latex wasn't available yet and the oil base paint vapors were tough to breathe. Within a twenty-four hour period, I painted the living room, dining room, kitchen, two foyers and three bedrooms. All the windows had been painted shut and I couldn't waste time unsealing them and so I painted until I began seeing things. When I saw a horse and carriage come down the stairway in the wee hours, I knew it was quitting time. We moved into the house a couple days before Christmas.

On day one, I was forcing open the upstairs window when I spotted Father Sullivan coming down the block. I felt he intended to surprise us and bless our home. We welcomed him and we all retreated to the kitchen for a tea break. He then disclosed his reason for the visit. He said Mrs. Moran, a parishioner, who had lived in the apartment house we just vacated, had passed away from cancer. Her husband recently had an operation and was unable to watch his children. He worked at Gate of Heaven Cemetery in Hawthorne as a gravedigger and needed someone to take care of his children during the week. Unfortunately, Mr. Moran had no money because he endured unbelievable expenses for medical treatment for his deceased wife. Furthermore, the church didn't have the finances and couldn't help much either. He asked Maureen and me if we could watch the children during the week. Mr. Moran would pick them up on Saturday morning and bring them back on Sunday evening. There were three children, John, who was nine years old, Gerry seven, and Mary Beth, five. I shuttered at the idea of taking in three children; after all, I was twenty-eight years old. Maureen was a year younger. I told Father Sullivan we couldn't handle it financially but he said the church would pay for their expenses. Desperate to get out of such a commitment, I reminded him that I didn't even have enough beds. He said he'd provide them. Maureen and I knew the children and we agreed to take them in on a temporary basis.

Father Sullivan sure blessed our house. He had a bounce in his canter when he departed from our house after his memorable visit.

Christmas was just around the corner. We had sent out cards, planned our first Christmas dinner at our house and invited the entire family. My brother, Larry, bought my son Denis a beautiful Collie pup and we named her Princess. We needed the dog like a hole in the head, but she was so smart and well behaved that she really wasn't a problem. That Christmas was indeed a special one. Despite the fact that we had nothing in the bank, we managed to get the kids an array of gifts. All of them were hurting over the loss of their mother and we tried to help them cope as much as we could.

We had a problem with the oldest son, John. He liked to play with matches. Once he set the curtains on fire. Fortunately, Maureen walked into the room in the nick of time and extinguished the flames. However, we gave all three of the children as much love as we could muster. To help with their money problems, I visited the doctor that Mrs. Moran frequented, Doctor Criares, who was also our physician. He was a good-looking bachelor and he had his share of young women as patients that I feel were healthy but really seeking a soul mate. The Morans, as I understood things, owed the doctor forty thousand dollars. Although I disliked begging, I went to see him. I had rehearsed in my mind many different ways of presenting my plea but when it came time, I merely said, "I'm here regarding the Moran Family. I understand Mr. Moran owes you a large sum of money, and, as you know, he is also sick." The good doctor left me in awe. He said, "Thanks for coming; based on the circumstances, tell him to forget about the bill." I was in awe and responded stupidly with, "Are you sure?" He confirmed what he said before asking me how I felt.

Doctor Criares was the first person to respond to a need such as this in my life but as you will find out, he was the first of many.

In those days, my food bills were enormous and the need for money was great. It was quite a chore doing the weekly shopping at Safeway on West 231 Street. I'd bring the kids with me to give Maureen a break. Customers stared at me with four children. In order to satisfy her curiosity one woman asked me at the checkout counter how old I was. Because it was rude of her to ask, I said, "Seventeen!" She was flabbergasted and I had a tough time holding it in.

Father Sullivan remained interested in the family's plight but the pastor expressed little or no interest. He never even visited us. Father Bell's focus in life was renovating the church with an expensive bell tower.

Fulfilling our commitment wasn't easy. Once, Mr. Moran, an immigrant from Ireland, came on Sunday evening to drop off the children. He was wasted and obviously spent the day drinking and not having quality time with his kids. Maureen also did his laundry but their clothes were filthy and they were hungry. I asked him to retreat to the basement as I had something to discuss with him. When we got there, the Marine Sergeant took control of me and I grabbed him by the neck and elevated his body until our eyes met. I told him if he ever had another drink when he was with the kids, I'd beat his ass so badly, he'd never be able to sit on a bar stool again. It's funny how fear can be an instant cure for alcoholism.

After a year and a half, the children's aunt and uncle bought a house in Wantagh and they moved. We had loved them dearly and their departure left us with mixed emotions. We were sad to see them leave but we now had an opportunity to do things that were impossible while they were with us.

Before they left, Maureen and I managed to bring people that came from County Kerry in Ireland together to solve the problem of bills the Morans still owed. We arranged to use the facilities at Gaelic Park on West 240 Street for a benefit dance. This was arranged through the owner, John Kerry O'Donnell, because he'd be providing the food and drinks he'd be making money on the affair. Progress was initially slow but improved drastically when they found out I wouldn't be holding the funds we'd collect. Over the years, I found out that immigrants don't trust "Yankees" with their money. Irish people in those days booked their travel at Grimes Travel

Agency, brought their meat at Kelly, the butcher, and banked at Emigrant Savings. At first I thought they were clannish but later realized that too many people in our culture are anxious to take advantage of immigrants. The businesses they frequented were trustworthy due to past experience and Irish involvement in their ownership. After our coming together with the people from County Kerry, the benefit dance went over well and a substantial amount of money was raised. It took care of the impending hospital bills.

Going though the experience of helping out the Morans was a gift from God. We realized that we had a mission to share the love we had for each other with the world around us. Children are the most vulnerable people in our society and we vowed to help them in any way we could, with the help of God.

While the Morans were still with us, we needed a car but couldn't afford one. My brother, Larry, said a friend was selling an old Chevy for only $25.00. He convinced me that I couldn't go wrong. Stupidly, I bought the car. It was rusted out and needed paint. I took my father-in-law in it to the local deli. He was thinking of painting it and fixing it up. He was already thinking of transportation to Port Jefferson. On the way, it went on fire. It didn't even survive the three-block drive. I managed to put out the flames but decided to junk it. I called a salvage yard and the guy on the phone was an unsympathetic smart ass. He said to drive it in and he'd give me twenty-five dollars. To tow it would cost me. I decided to drive it and he gave me the money and asked me to back it up for him. I told him the car can't go in reverse, smiled and departed. Bad luck to him!

We then bought a '54 Buick from a neighbor. At first, it was reliable transportation. We used it to go to Port Jefferson, Long Island almost every weekend. My father-in-law needed help building his house. He was a stubborn man and took advice from builders who didn't know their asses from their elbows. Most of our time was spent correcting their mistakes. Unfortunately, I had no experience in the building trade but I made up for it with sweat from hard work. There was plenty to shovel, mixing cement became routine and driving nails into studs became my specialty. Later in life, that experience helped me save money by doing things myself.

The Buick had charisma but due to a lack of knowledge about cars, it needed a battery and tune-up. This discovery was made on a cold winter morning. Triple A gave me a boost and told me to get a new battery. I drove to Sears on Fordham Road in the Bronx where they allegedly solved my problem. The next evening, it was deja-vous. After another boost, I arrived at Sears about an hour before closing. They waited on me about ten minutes before they closed their doors. They said they would have to verify that I needed a battery and I would have to leave the car. I reminded them that I had a new battery put in the car yesterday but he said, "It's your choice pal." I told him, he wasn't my pal and I shouted to the children in the car, "All of you can play with the tools when the bad man goes home in ten minutes." Needless to say, I was on my way with a new battery in five minutes. Bad luck to him!

If it's any consolation, Sears treats their customers better than their employees. I wonder if when they go belly-up, whether the government bails them out? I hope not!

There was one thing I loved about that old house. Maureen had fixed up my son Denis' room so perfectly. Another memory I have is my first father and son walk. Denis brought along a turtle that made strange noises. He called him "Charlie Knock-Knock." At the end of every block, we had a "hug session." He loved those squeezes almost as much as I did. We had a great time at the park and then I treated him to ice cream. As I often did, I prayed that the day would come when he would have his own child to love. Only then could he feel the same joy.

As he grew a little older, a little girl rang our bell one day. She was so small. I didn't see her when I opened the door but I heard her voice. The bottom of the storm door obstructed her image. It was a deep voice. She said it was Catherine, "Could Denis come out and play?" That was a nice neighborhood and we made many friends and it was so nice being so close to my mom and dad. We saw them every day. My mother used to stop in on every weekday and join Maureen and Denis with a cup of tea.

It was in 1965 when we found out that Maureen was expecting another baby. We were thrilled in knowing that we'd have another child in May. Everything was going well until Christmas time. We were stopped at a red light when we got hit in the rear. Fortunately, I had a blanket in the car. Maureen was hurt badly and I lifted her from the car and placed her on the blanket. Traffic was halted and the police responded. It was nice to feel their presence but nothing was happening. I asked them what was the problem?

I determined that Maureen was lying down on the line of demarcation between the 34th and 50th precincts. When I heard this, I pulled the blanket towards the 34th precinct and a responding ambulance took her to Jewish Memorial Hospital where our obstetrician practiced medicine. When we arrived, she was rushed into the emergency area where a doctor attended to her almost immediately. Although the wait probably took about a half hour, it seemed endless. Finally the doctor appeared. I rushed to him to determine how my wife was doing. He said, "I'm rather concerned due to the unusual swelling in her abdomen." I said, "You know she's pregnant!" He responded, "Oh, that's what it is!" At that time, Maureen's obstetrician made his appearance by entering a door about forty feet away. He yelled, "If you touch my patient, I'll kick your ass." Well, Maureen was hospitalized as a precaution; my son, Denis, and I decorated our Christmas tree without her that year. The lower branches were inundated with ornaments because my little man could only reach the lower branches. As he hung each bulb he'd inquire, "And doesn't that look nice?" Maureen was released from the hospital with stiffness and sores but managed to cook Christmas dinner for the entire family.

The bills were hard to meet in those days. Since we were in the proximity of Manhattan College, we advertised with them and rented out our basement. The only real encumbrance was an upright piano. It was determined that it probably played too many numbers but a fellow on my job expressed an interest in it and he made arrangements to pick it up. He was thrilled with the freebie and we were equally thrilled with the extra room it gave us.

Our two tenants were relatively well behaved. We didn't allow them to have sleep over guests or parties. We didn't have to press them to behave, they were aware that the powers to be at the college wouldn't condone any nonsense.

While we were at our first house we met with Father Peron. This was such a sad experience. He had been a missionary in Haiti. While he was there, Papa Doc (Francois Duvalier) came into power. Father Peron was a white man and he had to temporarily come to the United States until the dictatorship was terminated. Arrangements were made with the Archdiocese of Paris and the New York Archdiocese gave him an assignment in New York City. As ordered, he reported to the Chancery Office in

New York but was told to come back in two weeks. The bishop who was handling his case was on vacation. As I understand it, they were unsure he was a priest and dismissed him without further investigation. He couldn't communicate because he only spoke French. Therefore, he had no place to go and no money to get there. His choices were limited, so he slept at the Port Authority Bus Terminal, Pennsylvania Station, and Grand Central Terminal. In time he related to me how the police were overly aggressive in removing him and the other homeless bodies on several different occasions. Nobody seemed to care what was going to happen to them. Father Peron had an additional handicap; he didn't speak English. He could only communicate in French. He would eventually describe to me what it was like seeing the sizzling steaks being flipped in the windows of "Tads" in the midtown area. He said in his French accent that the saliva would drip on his shirt. During this time in his life, he didn't want to cast shame on the priesthood so he removed his roman collar as he begged on the sidewalks of New York.

After two weeks, he returned to the Chancery Office and with the intervention of God was sent to Our Lady of Visitation Parish in the Bronx. The pastor told him that he would have to be responsible for his own health insurance. He would be paid much less than the diocesan priests because he was still getting paid from the Archdiocese of Paris and after he got paid, took care of his medical insurance premium. After he had a haircut he had only a quarter left. He did have a roof over his head and three squares and fulfilled his priestly duty by saying Mass each morning. After he studied, he attempted to preach but the parishioners put up a stink because they had difficulty understanding him.

Maureen and I supported him as he formed "The League of Mary" in the parish. It was an organization that preached by example. We got involved with the lives of parishioners, identified their problems and did our best to solve or alleviate them. We also prayed together to the Blessed Mother and asked her to intervene in our work and she did.

At one point Father Peron expressed an interest in a car. He figured he could use it to visit friends he made in Haiti who immigrated to the United States. Maureen and I knew a parishioner who recently lost his wife, both of them had a car and now the widower only needed one. He donated the car to the church and it was given to Father Peron. Maureen taught him how to drive and he was excited over his anticipated inauguration drive to New Jersey. However, on the morning of his drive, the car went on fire ten feet before the sign welcoming everyone to the Garden State. Needless to say, the car was totaled but the insurance company gave him enough money to buy another cheap car.

Father Peron's English improved over time. One could understand him if they listened closely. We felt sorry for him. After all, he spent almost thirty years in a country that was so poor that their major exports were baseballs. He traveled throughout that country and had the luxury of only one coffee bean a day. He gave everything he had to the poor and now after being thrown out of Haiti, he was looked down upon by Christians who flaunted the name of Jesus but didn't live in accordance with the Gospel.

We decided to treat him to a nice dinner. He accepted our invitation readily. Maureen went to the enth degree. The dinner consisted of leg of lamb, which was marinated to perfection. We had a French onion soup to begin the meal and my surprise for him was an inexpensive bottle of wine from Burgundy, France, which was the area where he was raised. At the beginning of the meal, I poured the wine. After tasting it, a tear rolled down his cheek. We were concerned and asked him what was wrong. He said the wine was from his hometown in France. He hadn't tasted it in thirty years and now at an important juncture in his life, he had the opportunity to share the wine with good friends on his birthday. After dinner, he expressed his sadness in being separated from his friends in Haiti and he told us that he longed to be of greater value to God as a priest but was limited in what he could do because of language problems.

The next day, Maureen called her cousin, Father Frank Boyle, who married us. Frankie, as the family called him, had connections. He managed to arrange a transfer for Father Peron to Saint Vincent De Paul in lower Manhattan. This was probably the only French-speaking parish in New York City.

There were mixed emotions when he got word that he was being transferred. Communications with him after his departure indicated that he was doing well and was functioning very well in his ministry. He had no ill feelings over what happened.

He said he prayed for a safe return to the missions in Haiti. The memories of the miscommunications at the Chancery Office at the Archdiocese of New York, the two weeks he spent as a member of the homeless and the maggot he had for a pastor was just part of life as far as he was concerned. He felt his sufferings were nothing compared to Jesus Christ on the cross. This kind of forgiveness was unique, this kind of love was special, and his examples made me want to become a better person. His life definitely had a positive influence on me.

Graduation time came and we lost our tenants; but my mother's sister, Maggi (Margaret) came over from Ireland on a work visa. She paid us what we lost on the Manhattan College students but also joined us for breakfast and dinner. However, we considered it an act of charity. She was loved and filled in on rare occasions as a baby sitter whenever we needed one. We were saddened when she had to return to Ireland but found out that her daughter, who we called "Little Maggie" was approved for immigration. She was about seventeen and we were asked to look out for her.

She was no problem. She found a job quickly and paid her rent. She was no sandbagger! One night, she was driven home by a boyfriend whose name was John. I had met him before and he seemed to be a nice guy. However, he was "in the bag" that night. They were noisy and making out. I responded to the late hour party outside my front door. I ordered Little Maggie inside and John protested. She went inside the house but he decided to give me a push. I was less than tolerant and decked him. He spent the night sleeping in the hedge. They eventually got married and moved upstate. I was happy for them but they always held a grudge for my action that night. Many years later, I met her son. He had applied for a job with AAA where I was employed. While his application was pending, I asked him to have his mother give me a call but she never did. He never got the job. I wonder why?

On May 28, 1966 my second son was born. Maureen's pregnancy was one of concern due to the auto accident, but again we witnessed the power of prayer and God's presence in our lives. Padre Pio, a stigmatic and future saint was still alive in San Giovanni Rotunda, Italy. He was sent a card from Maureen imploring prayer on his part because the heartbeats of our baby at one point were not normal. We received a reply from a monk at his church advising us that Padre Pio wanted her to know that she would give birth to a healthy son.

Because Maureen spent seventeen hours in labor when Denis was born, she was adamant not to be hospitalized quite as long this time. She decided to have breakfast with my mom and eat all the things she was told not to. She told me the baby was about to be born but refused to go to the hospital. Finally, after her second cup of coffee, she said she was ready. I asked her, "Ready for what?" She said, "To have our baby." I grabbed the valise, which I had at arm's length and off we went to Jewish Memorial Hospital. Parking was always a problem there but I figured I'd find a spot when we got there but Maureen said, "The baby is coming now." I pulled into the service station opposite the hospital and the owner yelled, "You can't park there." I told him it was an emergency but he didn't care. Naturally, I ignored him and brought Maureen across the street. As we entered the hospital they immediately put her on a gurney and put her on an elevator destined to go to the maternity ward. At that moment, I saw Denis and Bea Moloney at the front door with looks of concern on their faces. I informed them of our early morning plight. Then I was told there was a phone call for me at the lobby reception desk. It was Dr, Hodge informing me that I was the father of a healthy, eight pound boy and Maureen, though now under anesthesia, did well with delivery "in the elevator."

I ran outside to the florist, got a large bouquet and raced with excitement to see her. It was impossible to wake her. All this joy and I couldn't share it with her.

At this time, I went to the nursery to see my son for the first time. I was behind a glass wall and the nurse was amid eight or ten babies. When she saw me, she lifted a baby and pointed to him as though he was mine. I motioned, "no" my baby, but she insisted and pointed to the sign on the incubator, "Baby Niland." I saw one of the most beautiful children with long red hair and gave thanks to God for entrusting this precious life in our care.

We now had two of our own children and since both of us were raised in New York City, we wanted to sell our house after five years and buy a house in the suburbs. We visited my brother in Saddle Brook and decided to look around that area.

Our shopping brought us to Paramus where we saw a bi-level for sale. It was new construction and we liked the area. The next day, I asked my brother to check it out. He called me to discuss his likes and dislikes and we finally realized he had gone to a different development. His description of a model, sugar maple split sounded better than the house we looked at; so we went there the next weekend and decided to buy one of the houses. It was more affordable; and we'd be only a block from a grammar school and a church, ten minutes from my brother Frank and fifthteen minutes from our parents. The commute to work would be on the Short Line bus and take ten minutes or so longer than by subway. The bus stop was only a one-block walk and the bus ticket was reasonable.

We needed a lawyer to help us close out the deal. My brother had used a Mr. Postman when he closed his house and because we didn't know any other lawyers in New Jersey, we hired him. He didn't strike us as being very impressive but did his job in a very competent manner. First, he suggested that we move along more quickly and he was able to secure a lesser interest rate for the mortgage. When he showed up at the contract signing, the sellers were shocked to see him. When they spotted him, one of them said, "Oh no! That son of a bitch!" Immediately, I knew I hired the right man for the job. Mr. Postman saved us money and did his job quickly and efficiently; when he showed up to sign contracts, he ripped the one they gave me and wrote his own with phrases favoring the buyer.

We used to travel to Paramus every weekend to observe how our house was progressing. The builder took a great pride in his work. He hired Europeans to do the work and paid them union wages. Many of them had gone through apprentice programs in their home country. They were pleasant and competent. Once the interior of the house was painted, we were banned from entering it. The builder, Mr. Richie Wells, said that in the past, future owners put handprints on the walls and blamed him. Therefore, we had to wait for the big day. We understood and wanted our new house to be perfect, although, we couldn't afford to get anything extra. The cost of a fireplace was $700 and an extra garage $750. Baseboard heating would have cost $900. We were satisfied with the basics.

Finally, the house was ready. My mother cried knowing that we were moving to New Jersey. You'd swear that we were going to Australia. We made our big move in February 1968. It was sad leaving our old neighborhood and saying goodbye to the friends we made. It wasn't easy but the future for our children seemed brighter and that's what was important to us. The mortgage payments seemed reasonable and we felt we'd have no financial problems.

I'll never forget the day when we walked into the house for the first time.

The hardwood floors glistened, and the pristine white walls were beckoning us to make ourselves at home. We thanked God for this gift and appreciated the fact that this was a far cry from the apartments where we were raised.

That was one of the only days in my life when I woke up with an ache in the lumbar region of my back. However, I did manage to move everything out of my other house, a building that served us well. My brothers and father-in-law were a big help that day. Maureen insisted on privacy and my last chore that night was putting up curtains on the picture window. My back was so sore; I fell off the ladder and broke the largest pane of glass.

My next chore was reporting the damage to my insurance company. When I called, they said my policy had been mailed. I told them I was calling because I had a claim. Naturally, I was upset about the window but I had joy reporting the claim. I detest insurance companies, oil companies, and banks but not necessarily in that order. As far as I'm concerned, they operate like foreign countries and will chisel you out of your last penny if they could. Bad luck to all of them!

7

THE AUTOMOBILE CLUB OF NEW YORK

When I started working at the Automobile Club of New York, the Board of Directors consisted of responsible and well-respected individuals. The benefits were extraordinary. You could retire after twenty years of service, upon the approval of the Board of Directors. After ten years, each employee received an annuity worth thirty-five percent of their ten year salary and which matured after ten years. Another policy was given after fifteen years for sixty-five percent of their salary and another after twenty years of service, worth one hundred and twenty percent of their twentieth year's salary.

A Christmas bonus representing one percent for each year of longevity accompanied a special bonus, which was usually fifteen percent. These benefits wilted away. The Auto Club got fatter at the top as turnover increased.

When an employee started in the travel department, he or she was rated as a Junior Counselor and trained in marking trip-tiks (a book of AAA maps). One could mark one hundred of these accurately in a week, and could work overtime and receive compensation at time and a half. As the need arose, counselors were transferred to branch offices and telephone work. A counselor could take the annual Senior Counselor's test when they felt qualified. By doing so they could increase their salary substantially. The more junior you were, the greater the increase would be.

After a short time, another counselor named, Marty, and I took the test and passed it. It required at least three hours of study, every night for a whole year. We immediately doubled our salary and made it more lucrative to work overtime. During the summer travel season I'd work my regular eighty hours in two weeks along with one hundred and twenty hours of overtime. This is how Maureen and I purchased our first house.

Is it any wonder that after two years, I was promoted to Assistant Supervisor in the Telephone Travel Department and after another year or so to Supervisor?

Early in my career, the retirement was modified. A realistic plan was devised to supplement anticipated Social Security payments.

Initially, the executives were well-respected individuals. Unfortunately, an ex-Sanitary Engineer named Charles Murphy was made Director of Travel. When I was a new supervisor, he demanded an evaluation on each of my fifty-two members of staff. He mandated that I rate them according to their value to the company. He then asked me to make a case against the ones at the bottom. He was ruthless! He also mandated that I give a quiz to all the travel management personnel, mark each test for accuracy and report directly to him. It was my job, but it was difficult as a rookie supervisor to scrutinize a member of management with years of seniority. Furthermore, these were men I had worked with and respected. Charlie Murphy didn't care. He was a modern day Simon Legree and a first-class maggot; his scrupulous antics helped him rise to the position of President. His was a reign of fear.

The day came when his son was also employed as a management trainee. He was a real numb–nut, but with his magical DNA and nepotism supreme, was promoted to Assistant Supervisor in no time at all. Wouldn't you know it; he then got promoted to Supervisor but had no staff and no obvious responsibility. Finally, he got promoted to Assistant Director in record time and there was a revolution on the Board of Directors. That day, it was announced that Charlie was gone, "bad luck to him," and his son with him. I felt sure there was a sweet severance package.

We then found out that the Club had a new President. His name was Harold Meyers. I hardly knew him but he had pre-conceived notions of me and was my enemy from day one. No one respected this ogre. He had a background in public relations but lacked charisma.

Although my performance was rated as superb, he was determined to fire me. It is my feeling that his cronies, regardless of my concern and hard work, had sorely misinformed him. His rating system was based on what you could do for him personally. One guy named Larry, painted his house and lent him money. This earned him a promotion to Assistant Director and boy, did the power go to his head!

One day, I made a decision that he disagreed with. He called me into his office and yelled at me. I told him it wasn't necessary to raise his voice, I could hear him. With this, he became livid and said "If you ever do anything like this again, I'll punch you in the mouth." I couldn't believe my ears. I told him if he raised his hand at me, I'd throw him through his window and park his ass on Seventh Avenue. I then inquired, "Will that be all?" With sweat rolling down his brow and a quiver in his voice, I felt I stopped an up and coming Hitler in his tracks. What a maggot! Bad luck to him!

His assistant, a man whose job I once saved from Charlie Murphy's Evil Empire, walked through my operation one day and said, "It's about time you guys got a new Christmas tree." My staff related to his comment and I felt compelled to get a new tree and I did. The expense, about twenty-five dollars, or about fifty cents per staff member, was put on a petty cash voucher and submitted to my Director, Frank Siragusa. He informed me this was a personal decision and I would have to bear the expense. It was my decision to buy the tree. Things surely were petty and I saw the tide was against me. I told him since it was considered my tree, I'd bring it back to Woolworth's and get my money back. This rattled everyone from the President down; I couldn't believe the poor quality of management at the Club. Making the staff happy was not a priority for them, I was told to do nothing and Frank would get back to me. The next day, I'd guess after a night of power broking; I was told that Mr. Meyers would chip in, he would chip in, my assistants would be asked to chip in and pay for the tree. I told him this was unsatisfactory. My assistants were Jewish and the Christmas tree had nothing to do with their holiday. I told him to tell Mr. Meyers what he could do with his two dollars. They decided to pay for the tree. Later a Jewish member of staff asked if we could have a menorah. I said Mr. Siragusa must approve such requests. He did and he sent his secretary out to buy one; I wondered if the Auto Club paid for it. I suspect they did.

Because of their poor management, employees attempted to form a union. The first vote was a tie and the latter vote was in the favor of the Club by a very small margin. I believe it was one vote.

Once, I was called to the office of the President. I had no idea what this would be about but I knew I wasn't going to be happy over an encounter with the great Harold Myers. As I entered the office he immediately held up what appeared to be a letter in his hand and told me correspondence was received that mentioned my name and several other members of management. The anonymous letter said we were "screwed" by the Club. He wanted to know why I wrote the letter. I told him I didn't. He then said my wife must have written it. I told him she didn't. He continued to be persistent and seemed to be convinced that I was the culprit. No matter what I said, I couldn't change his mind. I knew I had to make a strong statement that would make him realize that he was wrong. I told him that the handwriting on the letter that he was holding in his hand didn't come close to resembling my writing or Maureen's. Furthermore, it appeared to me that the person who wrote it must be an illiterate. The scribbling was not mine. He responded with this comment, "Joe, these are my notes!"

Everyday, I was constantly criticized by upper management. However, I managed to stay focused on my duties as supervisor. Overtime was down and sales were up. Training was at an all time high. The staff was motivated and I kept the attitude upper management had towards me to myself. Unfortunately, two of my assistants, were in daily communications with my bosses; I reminded them every day that they were back stabbers and I knew what they were doing. . There was no loyalty on their part, but I rode the wave.

The Board of Directors was vindictive and stupid. Once I received a mandate to prepare fifty-two evaluations within a two-week period of time along with running the day-to-day operation. I recognized this as an assignment they felt I couldn't handle and one that could have serious repercussions. Therefore, I dictated all of them and tied up four secretaries. As soon as I got one back, I'd correct it and resubmit it. There were no computers in those days. Finally, they told me that they were giving me another two weeks. I told them it wasn't necessary but they cried that they had priorities that had to be handled. They had no chutzpa.

One day, I was called into the office of Frank Siragusa. He told me they had received their monthly phone bill and determined that I abused the privilege. I admitted to calling my wife each day as I was leaving the office so she could plan dinner. He said that others in my position don't find this necessary. I told him I would stop doing this and leave everyday at 5:00 PM as they did. He knew I frequently stayed late and backed off. However, he pointed out that on one day, I spent forty-five minutes on the phone with my wife and he showed me the call he was referring to on the phone bill. I couldn't recall and apologized. He chastised me for not recalling speaking to my wife at such great length. Finally, he had something to report to the President. I returned to my operation shaking my head. And then it hit me, Jim Lyons, my maggot assistant, didn't know what the hell he was doing on a Sunday afternoon and called me for advice and assistance. This was the call Frank was referring to. I went back to his office and informed him accordingly. He responded, "That's a moot point." It was then when I saw the handwriting on the wall. A week or so later, I was called into the President's office. I was told that a decision was made to terminate me. I asked why, I was told, "It's time for a change." I was also told that if I wished, I could see Tony Ippolito, the Director of Emergency Road Service. If he had a job for me, it was solely up to him. I knew the way they worked. One of their flunkies got my job and Tony knew the quality of my work and hired me as a field representative with a drop in salary. In one day I went to being a so-called expert in the travel business to a dummy in the Road Service Department. I didn't even know how to tune up a car but it was a time for humility. There were mouths to feed.

I learned the job quickly. One day I was out on the Grand Concourse in the Bronx. After I stopped, I got rammed from behind. Despite the pain, I had the stamina to keep working. About six months later, I was stopped on Hillside Avenue in Jamaica. I was awaiting the opportunity to make a left turn when I got hit from behind by a gypsy cab. This time I was really hurting and was hospitalized. I had damaged some of my cervical discs.

Now I was involved in a compensation case. I sued the person who hit me along with the Auto Club. I wanted job security and I wanted them to realize that they couldn't fire me without liability because I was injured on the job. They showed initial concern. They even visited me in the hospital but when I sued them, they became distant and cold like the good ole' days.

I didn't rush back to work. My spirit to do a good job was hampered and my survival skills kicked in. As I returned, I was in no shape to drive so I performed my job on the phone, being bent over my desk. My boss at the time was a bright draft dodger with a superiority complex. He had no sense of humor and I found it humorous seeing him lose it at least once a day. However, he had a better degree of intelligence than the people I dealt with in travel. He wasn't incompetent but was in contention for having one of the foulest mouths at the Club. His name was Lou Fiorito.

Of all jobs, they also had me handle complaints from members. I felt confined in the office but managed to laugh from time to time. Once there was a clock on the wall that no longer worked and so I ordered a replacement. I took the old clock and sent it to Marty Grossman, a field rep, and told him the paper work would follow. It was a special complaint I was handling for the President. For six months, he drove with the clock in the back seat. Finally, he was dispatched by radio to pick up Lou Fiorito. As he entered the back seat, he saw the clock with my notes on it. He demanded him to stop the car. He got out and in a rage and smashed the clock on Seventh Avenue. Later, he returned to the office and chewed me out. I guess I deserved that one.

On another day, he was well dressed for a meeting and when he got out of the car at the garage fell on an oil slick. I got a call from the garage telling me not to laugh when he entered the office. I giggled as silently as I could at my desk as I overheard him cursing and swearing behind his desk. He didn't respond to my cheery "Good Morning."

After taking a drop in pay, I went to the local Community College and passed my test to be a Real Estate Agent. I wouldn't work an extra minute for AAA so I sold houses to supplement my salary.

These were the days of heavy drug use in the late sixties and early seventies. One of the Emergency Road Service shifts was riddled with drugs and nothing was being done about it. Service was going downhill and nobody had the courage to face the music. The druggies were running the institution. Everyone that was offered a promotion turned down the job. They faced a dilemma. What they needed was a Marine Corps Sergeant to run the shift. They asked me to accept the assignment and I told them I would if they restored my pay and promoted me and they did. The sentence was for one year. I realized the hours were difficult but again I reminded myself that I had mouths to feed. My wife and children were the priority in my life.

I was told that I would report to the ERS Director, Ed Miller as usual, but anything relating to drugs would be conveyed by me to Mr. Ippolito only. Mr. Miller would not be told of any drug related incident. This alienated him but I didn't care. He was the man overseeing ERS, drinking his lunches when the druggies carried on. Besides, I hate drugs with a passion and was a natural for this job.

On my first day as the shift supervisor, a young lady named Tina informed me that there was a young man on the shift and everyone was afraid of him. I asked her why. She said he carries a knife and is the one that's been cutting up the chairs. He had already threatened members of the staff with his knife. I thanked her for calling this matter to my attention. To set the mood for my regime as Supervisor, I casually called him into the office and told him in a very private discussion that I wanted him to quit. Looking at him eyeball to eyeball with my hand on his neck, I invited him to pull his knife and I'd shove it up his ass. The staff was surprised when they heard of his sudden and unexpected resignation.

On another night, I said hello to the staff in the lounge and smelled pot. I lined up my suspects in four different offices and corners and interrogated them. It took about an hour before they all confessed. I called Tony Ippolito and got the okay to fire them all.

On one incident, members were calling back because they never received service and we had no records of the calls. This was pre-computer, which meant that someone was throwing the requests for service in the garbage. I went to each radio channel and emptied the trash baskets on the tabletops. At one location I observed the missing requests. The maggot stormed out and never returned. I didn't have to say a word. Bad luck to him! About a year later, he and his brother were involved in bludgeoning an old lady to death.

To clearly illustrate how the inmates were in control, one young man was caught by me mixing a gin and tonic at his workstation.

As I reported for work early one night, I answered the phone. The caller told me the next time I took out the garbage would be my last. I told him that I didn't accept threatening phone calls until my shift officially began. Threats were also conveyed to the Board of Directors and they actually hired a guard wielding a shotgun to observe what was going on and to walk me to my car at the end of each day. I'm sure their primary concern was liability. They couldn't have cared less about me.

On one occasion, I requested far in advance to have a Sunday off. I had accrued the time. I explained that I was going to a baptism and I was officiating at the rite as a Deacon. I was also going to become the godfather for another employee's daughter. Ed Miller refused my request and said I'd be fired if I didn't show up for work. I went to the baptism but had to leave during the reception. I felt terrible that I also had to work on the day of Ed Miller's funeral.

One of the fringe benefits that still existed was a gold clock, which was presented on an employee's twenty-fifth anniversary. It was more than bad luck when this procedure was discontinued when it was my turn to receive this gift.

Service was improved and all the druggies were gone. As agreed, they transferred me to a different shift and my hours were much better.

Interestingly enough, our President, Harold Meyers, hired his genius son. He was put in charge of the telephone and computer network after making a nuisance of himself elsewhere. One night, during a storm, we had problems with computers. They operated on waves and because they added a floor on a skyscraper on the eastside, the signals were disrupted. He couldn't figure out the problem. He called me and asked me to look out the window and determine if our disc on the Hotel Pierre was damaged. I told him the weather was so bad that I couldn't see across the street. He then asked me to have a younger person with good eyesight, look for possible damage. I put him on hold and when I returned I told him I saw the problem. He asked what it was and I told him it was a slipped disk. He didn't appreciate my humor. He responded, "Ha ha, I don't think that's very funny."

When his father left the Club, Warren Meyers also resigned. I'm sure his future wasn't as promising as it was at one time. I was told that he got a job in Australia and even that wasn't far enough away. Bad luck to him!

Interesting enough, when the old man was at the Club, he was always chauffeured and never drove. I had my suspicions. Whatever the answer, I felt it would have cast a shadow on an organization that prides itself on safe driving.

As the years went on, the road service and travel departments merged. At one time I was banned from travel but now I was part of it again and a knowledgeable member at that.

Before I retired, they asked me to manage our Newburgh Office. I was there from day one, hired and trained the staff and when I left there were ninety employees and the operation was running smoothly. The woman they hired to be my sidekick was promoted to Assistant Director. Naturally, I asked them why I wasn't offered the job, knowing well that they never forgave me for suing them. The response was, "You're not in our future." Actually, I did want not to be there anymore.

I discussed briefly some of the incidents in my career at Triple A because it was a well-run business with satisfied employees when I first started working there. Then greed affected those in command in this not for profit business. Change could have occurred by members voting for a new Board but most people don't bother, as you well know. The sons who inherit responsible positions are oftentimes incompetent and almost always overrate their own performance. If it weren't for National Headquarters policing the Auto Club of New York, they would have gone belly up.

It was sad that I worked for such mean people but the staff was overwhelmingly pleasant and because of them, I enjoyed the job. It is a tense situation when you're asked to make a case on someone they want fired, it's a shame when you are held in less regard because you don't go drinking with the boys and it's difficult to witness wholesale nepotism.

As my job moved from place to place, the commute was awkward, time consuming and expensive but Maureen and I didn't live for things we didn't need, luxuries we had no need for and we didn't allow our children to fall into such a trap.

We all have to work for a living. Maybe my father was right when he said to get a civil service job. Then again, I enjoyed the challenge of learning and leading people. Maybe they didn't like me but when Joan Rivers wanted a travel expert on her show, they called on me. Somebody had to get the job done while they were having long expensive luncheons and vacations on the member's fees.

By the way, there were many who got shafted. Don't believe me; it's all in that anonymous letter. I wish I knew who wrote it. I'd buy them dinner for making Harold Myers quiver in his boots.

Things improved when Don Phillips became President. His wife was extremely competent and extremely hated. Vice Presidents cried on my shoulder when she got on their case. She would not condone them mistreating staff and strived for a well run Auto Club. After her husband passed away, she resigned. I wonder why? Now back to my home in Paramus.

8

OUR HOME IN PARAMUS

Aside from the three model houses, ours was the first one built in our development and we were the first family to move in. Once a celery farm, the area was now referred to as Deer Trail Farms. An elderly man was subcontracted to do the landscaping. One day, as he was riding his tractor, he fell off and was being dragged. Maureen spotted this from the kitchen window. She recognized his emergency and rushed to his aid. She climbed aboard the runaway machine applied the brakes and turned off the ignition. She then called the police and he received emergency medical attention. Again, my wife saved a life but thought nothing of it. This was our first encounter with the Paramus Police, but not our last.

One day at work, one of our employees, Mary Jo Davis, had a severe headache. I sent another employee with her to the emergency room of a nearby hospital. Later in the day, Mary Jo called me. She said her malady was diagnosed. She had an arterial aneurysm and it was inoperable. The doctor told her she would die within hours. In the interim, her headache was intolerable. I rushed to the hospital to convey my sympathy and to ask if there was anything I could do. She said that there was no one to care for her Afghan Hounds, Sally and Athena. They were provided for in her will but her friend, Danny Montoro, was on his way up from Florida to tend to their needs. Naturally, I agreed to care for them until Danny was able to assume this duty.

Mary Jo was an interesting character. She was one of many employees Maureen and I socialized with. She hated the Eastside of New York. She felt the people who lived there were frauds of the worst kind. She made it a point to live in a garden apartment on the Westside around Ninetieth

Street. At times our parties there got noisy and the neighbors threw eggs at us. She casually invited us under one of several patio umbrellas to avoid direct hits.

Her husband didn't work. He stayed at home and painted. His art was displayed in their apartment. I admired one of his so-called masterpieces to be polite, but actually, I couldn't stand it. He offered it to me as a gift. Naturally, I told him I couldn't accept it but thanked him for his kind gesture. His paintings were abstract and frequently had objects such as springs and paper clips protruding from them.

He eventually took his own life and willed his paintings to the Vatican. I told Maureen they were probably displayed in the catacombs. Someone informed her that they were worth a fortune. Nevertheless, I would not have hung any of his paintings in my house.

Mary Jo was about thirty-five and was alleged to be the sole heir of the Gorham Silver Company. She didn't get along with her family and lived away from all of them. She was world traveled, spoke French and Italian, and dabbled heavily in the stock market. She always gave me good tips but I had no money to invest.

She was full of life and very popular with the staff. She worked evenings only, frequented Broadway plays, and went on every educational tour that the Auto Club offered to her.

All these memories flashed through my head after she succumbed to her medical malady and I proceeded home with two of the weirdest looking dogs on the back seat of my new Dodge Dart. They sent shivers up my spine whenever I looked in the rearview mirror and saw them gaping at me with their heads so erect.

They were put in the basement of my house. I didn't want them to cause any destruction upstairs. There was nothing in the basement that they could mess up. The only things there were a ping-pong table and a big roll of lamp wick the plumbers had left. At about three in the morning, there was a high-pitched whining sound. I had no idea what it was but I rushed downstairs to see what was wrong.

About a foot over the ping-pong table was Sally. Her body was wrapped like a mummy as she swung back and forth over the table. It appeared the animals were playing with the lamp wick. Somehow it got above the supports between the beams of the ceiling and she became helplessly trapped.

Athena sat motionless with a dumb look on her face. It seemed like brain surgery cutting the twine away from a dog's body, which was the same color. Furthermore, as I removed more and more twine, she tried biting me in fear but the operation was a success.

The next morning, I walked those dogs outside the house. All of the construction equipment stopped and the machine operators heckled in wonder as I walked two of the ugliest animals on the face of planet earth. I didn't appreciate their comments but I had heard worse in my day.

It was sad seeing Mary Jo, a good friend, buried in the prime of her life. All of her stock holdings, investments and knowledge were left behind in a world that merely prepares us for the real reason we are here.

We had many friends at the Auto Club and we had them as guests at our home whenever we could afford to do so. Many of them were gay. We didn't think they were freaks, we thought they were kind and thoughtful. We loved visiting their homes. They were great decorators and great people. One of them left our AAA Travel Department and opened a gay travel agency in San Francisco. This was during a time when gays weren't socially accepted, but he defied the odds and did well. He had a great sense of humor, knew many people, and had the initial money necessary for the business world.

It was our feeling that they should be treated properly in society. The subject of same sex marriage wasn't introduced to society; if it was, Maureen and I wouldn't have approved of it. However, they shouldn't be deprived of any benefits.

One day, Maureen was invited to visit the Edna B. Conklin home for children. It was a residence reserved for children who were wards of the State of New Jersey. Some were orphans seeking adoption and others looking for foster homes. She was devastated over children not having a mother or father to care for them; so we went to Bergen Pines Hospital in Paramus and had a complete health examination to be approved as foster parents. We paid for the medical exams and that didn't seem right.

We then were interviewed by recently graduated social workers that didn't know their asses from their elbows. I'm sure they did well with textbooks but they didn't exercise any discretion. Maureen had me promise not to ask any difficult questions for them to answer and we were accepted as foster parents.

Our first foster child was a young boy named Paul. He was about three years old but had superior intelligence. He was available for adoption. We weren't in a position to adopt but we said we'd give him a home until suitable parents were found.

Paul was a handsome tyke. He was about the same age as my son, Brian. He had jet-black hair and eyes that looked like black olives. I used to give him a Baby Ben Alarm Clock and toy screwdriver to play with. He could take it apart and put it back together as he sat in his high chair. He couldn't tell time but when he set off the alarm, he knew his endeavor was a success. Paul was with us for about six months. We were told two doctors adopted him. Paul is a physician today.

The first neighbors we met in Paramus were the Froms. They had been farmers and at one time owned a large tract of land where the Paramus Post Office is located. They sold their property and bought the model home in our development. Joe was at one time the Grand Marshall in our Independence Day Parade and a respected member of the community. His wife, Jeanne, was born in the United States, was raised in Poland and returned to America as a young woman. The Froms had three daughters. Only one of them was going to elementary school, the others had graduated high school and were attending college. Joe spent most of his time tending bar in Paterson. This was a business venture he pursued when he sold his farm. However, he still did farming in the back of his house, boasted about his fishing, and enjoyed frequenting the Elks.

He was the annual chairman of Polish Night at the Elks and took pride in how well it was run. He was a generous soul and made golden friendships over the years. Because of Joe, I joined the Elks and one day he approached me and asked if I would be on his committee for Polish Night. I reminded him that I was Irish and knew nothing about Polish traditions or likes or dislikes of Polish people. He said he only needed someone he could trust to take care of the tickets and the money. I agreed to do it for him.

About a week later, Joe had a heart attack and was in the intensive care unit of the hospital. I went to visit him. I told him how concerned I was and I told him if there was anything I could do, I would. He said there was something I could do; be the Chairman of Polish Night at the Elks. Because of the wonderful friendship we had, I agreed.

Since Polish Night was coming soon, I had to make plans. There were a group of Polish members who always wanted to run this festive occasion but Joe knew of their jealousy and stopped them from their plight by having me run the affair. This way Joe would again have the honor the following year.

I didn't have all the contacts that Joe had for running this affair so I wasn't getting the usual cooperation. Because I had no Polish heritage, I thought of something unusual. I approached a young man named Stanley Pelc who was the leader of a dance troupe of sixteen. They performed at Lincoln Center in home-made costumes. These clothes were elaborate and they were like those worn by Polish People in different parts of their mother country. Their dancing was culturally rich and a cinch to be a hit. He told me that each dancer brings four outfits and they charge $600 for the performance.

My dance committee consisted of several friends of Joe From and my brother. I presented the possibility of hiring the dancers and asked for a show of hands. My brother and I raised our hands. I asked them what they didn't like about my suggestion. The answer was unanimous; it cost too much!

Naturally, I contacted Stanley and told him what had transpired. He said he would look into a possible alternative and that would be to have only half of them perform at half the price. I thanked him and a short time later he was able to confirm such an arrangement. Again, I went before the committee. Again, my brother, Frank and I were the only ones with hands raised. Again, the answer was unanimous; it cost too much!

I called Stanley and told him the bad news. I told him that it would have been a wonderful thing for the attendees if they performed. As a last ditch effort, I asked if they would perform for the sake of promoting Polish culture. He said he'd look into this remote possibility.

Surprisingly, they agreed; all we had to do is feed them. Now, I went before the committee and facetiously said, "Who is in favor now?" Everyone raised their hand except for Stefan Kanupka. I asked him why he wasn't in favor of our plan. He said, "I hope they don't eat too much."

Well Polish Night at the Elks was a smash and the dancers were invited back in years to come with pay.

I made many friends at the Elks and was impressed with the work that they performed for needy children.

Maureen and I added to our family with our son, John. All of our sons are beautifully different and loveable. Like most parents, we wanted the best for them.

We took in many foster children in those days, and we took in runaways that were brought to us by the Juvenile Division of the Paramus Police. Captain Al Smith was the officer that showed a special concern for teenagers who had trouble in their lives. He believed in kids. His partners Richie DeAngelo and Gunther Klink were also devoted to the needs of children.

There was a common denominator among these children. They always told me that their parents never told them that they loved them. Because of this, whenever I worked late and my children were in bed when I got home, I'd go to their room and grab them by the back of the head, look them in the eyes and tell them that I love them. They always managed a tired smile of contentment and I always prayed in thanksgiving to God for entrusting them in my care. To this day, when they are among adult friends and I'm departing, I say, "Good-bye, I love you."

The Division of Youth and Family Services wasn't too sharp in those days. The money given to foster parents was miniscule and worse yet, the case follow-up was horrendous. Maureen and I knew we should do something about it, but we were helpless because we didn't have the names and addresses of foster parents. Therefore, we were unable to communicate with them. We all needed one voice, but the State was unwilling to cooperate and dreaded the thought of us being able to communicate with each other.

The records of all the foster parents in Bergen County were secured the same way the Marine Corps secured the M-1 rifle, by moonlight requisition. We mailed letters to all of them and planned the first meeting of the Foster Parents of Bergen County on December 9, 1970. We were feeling very optimistic but on that day my mother passed away. Naturally, I was busy with the funeral arrangements but begged Maureen to attend the meeting. I couldn't disregard the rendezvous because we had put so much effort into it and it was so meaningful for the children and parents.

Maureen attended and ran the meeting, as I knew she would. The foster parents weren't greedy for money. They were concerned about the cost of food and clothes. We promised to follow up on their concerns and we addressed them to the Director of DYFS together with our personal concerns. However, we felt confident nothing would be done and if that were the case, our concerns would become demands. It was impossible to talk to a DYFS worker without them telling you how busy they were, how underpaid they were, and how unhappy they were with their bosses. Their concern was always for themselves. I always felt that a good caseworker would have had to be in the same boat as the children they're supposed to serve but if that was the case, they were then usually incompetent because of the mental anguish they endured in their childhood.

We felt we had a solution regarding the cost of clothes. If we had a place to meet and exchange clothes, it would be like money in the bank. I approached the head person at the Elks and asked if we could use their hall once a month. They were more than happy to do it and we picked a date. Foster parents came by the droves that afternoon. Many of us made new friends and poor but loving foster parents walked away with clothes for their children.

The next day, I got word that the powers that be at the Elks wanted a word with me. When I arrived, I could tell by the looks on their faces that something was wrong. They told me that I would no longer be able to use their hall for a clothing exchange. I asked why. They said they had too many commitments requiring the use of the hall. I asked them, "What kind of commitments? However, they couldn't name any. I asked them what prompted our meeting and they said several members complained. I asked what the gist of their complaints was. They said it was the caliber of the people attending. At that time, it hit me. Many poor Blacks and Hispanics tainted lily-white Paramus. They acknowledged I was right with their gestures but they were afraid to admit it verbally. I told them that they were all maggots and told them I quit the Elks. Admittedly, I gave them some gestures of my own and told them I wouldn't give them the steam off my piss. I never graced their doors again as a member.

I understand that the Elks have changed their image, but as far as I'm concerned, they passed over that imaginary line and must pay for the sins of their fathers.

Around this time, I was struggling to get legislation passed regarding the adoption laws in New Jersey. After many referrals, I contacted the Grand Knight of the Knights of Columbus' phone number but I was told he was conducting other business. I was asked to call back at another time. Well, I did call back many times, but to no avail. Finally, I called and he apparently answered the phone by accident. I barely had a chance but told him we could use a letter of support. I contacted him because of the great work the Knights do for children. He said, "We don't have time for such bullshit." I told him that I would never become a member of the Knights of Columbus because of this incident. Whenever, anyone asks me to join; I will tell him that they don't know how to pick their leaders and I will reiterate the conversation we had. Finally, I told him he was a maggot as he slammed the phone in my ears.

Over the years, I was asked many times to become a Knight and I told the story to unwilling listeners. A friend once asked me what it would take to become a Knight and after a lengthy discussion, I agreed to join if they named the local council after a parish priest at Annunciation Church who was awarded the Congressional Medal of Honor posthumously for his valor in Vietnam. His name was Reverend Charles Watters.

The name change took place and I joined. Now I am a proud fourth degree member of the Knights of Columbus. It was an act of humility and a reminder for me how thick-headed I can be at times. You can't always judge good organizations by a few bad men but there are times when your conscience calls upon you to stand up and be counted.

Today, I hold both the Knights of Columbus and the Elks in high regard. Their leadership is outstanding in Paramus and they devote many hours of their time helping the oppressed and disadvantaged. May God bless them for all the good they do.

It is my strong recommendation for young people to join these organizations and select good leaders. If they do, their membership will grow and if anyone crosses that imaginary line step forward and call on your peers within the organization to make the right decisions.

9

A REVOLTING DEVELOPMENT

Things got very busy in our household. Many of the foster parents called Maureen regarding their problems with children. They would rather get advice from her than from a case worker who really didn't have the time because of their "case load."

In any case, children weren't checked up on if they were in an established home with a good reputation; but how about a phone call once a month? After we started up the Foster Parents Association we were in a position to refer foster parents to another family with appropriate clothes sizes. Furthermore, we felt we were instrumental in getting necessary monetary increases for foster parents from the State of New Jersey.

In the midst of all the turmoil, we received a call from a nun who said she was concerned that thirty-six children in temporary residence at the Jersey City Medical Center were not being taken care of properly. In a quest for the truth, Maureen and I went there but we were denied access and couldn't visit the children.

Maureen didn't take no for an answer. She went with the nun one evening and climbed the fire escape and determined that the help was far from adequate. Many of the children were not toilet trained and had to lay in their own feces and urine. It was so disheartening to become aware of this abuse; so we decided to do something about it.

We had made some wonderful friends in the press. People like Al Capp, the cartoonist, and Mark Stewart of The Record. They, along with others, picked up on the story and all of a sudden it made newspaper headlines in the local news. It was at this time that we began to get threatening phone calls from an unknown source. The calls came from several individuals and at all hours. No one would identify who he or she was or whom they represented. They told us that we were all going to be wiped out if we didn't cool it. They didn't want us to utter another comment to the press regarding these children. It was clear that an actual contract had been put out on my entire family. We couldn't figure out what we had done to warrant their attention.

A good friend with "inside" connections verified that we had dug a big hole for ourselves. I felt helpless, especially when I found a hole in my storm door resembling that of a round from a weapon. However, I searched far and wide and couldn't find a bullet. It must have been a manufacturing defect that went unnoticed when the door was installed, but it gave me something to think about. I kept that door for years as a reminder that Christ and the Blessed Mother approved of our work. Naturally I prayed for an answer for the impending question.

Because I live a charmed life and God looks favorably upon me, I picked up a newspaper and saw a familiar person. When I was a teenager, I used to go to Palisades Amusement Park by bus. When I got there, my buddy, Dooley, and I used to check discarded packs of cigarettes at the bus terminal for loose change. Smokers threw away their empty packs and money that had been carelessly thrown in their pockets. The loose change had found its way into the cigarette packs. We also found bent and stale butts, which we smoked.

We were almost always broke and couldn't spend much time on the rides but we always found time to talk to the young man at the concession stand where you throw the ball to knock down the metal bottles. He was an immigrant from Italy. I'd guess he was in his thirties. His name was Gus and he spoke with a gruff accent. We found him to be an interesting guy and a nice person. He had plenty of time to chat because business was slow during those hot summer days.

Wouldn't you know it? I believed that the person I read about in an article in the daily newspaper was this same Gus that I had met at Palisades Park years ago. The news article indicated that he had just made a sizeable donation to the Dominican Nuns at an orphanage in Rockland County. It was my belief that this was a person of influence and was now a Commissioner of Parks for one of the towns along the Hudson River.

Maureen agreed with me that I should contact him and see if he'd have some influence with the right people, not only to make the death contract go away but to alleviate the serious problem these orphans and wards of the State were experiencing.

The next thing I did was to call him. I attempted to verify that he was the same person. It was now many years later and the person I spoke to had a much gruffer voice but I felt sure it was him. However, he wasn't interested in reminiscing as much as he wanted to know what was on my mind.

He told me that he didn't do business over the phone but I could go to his restaurant in North Bergen and discuss it with him. I had no choice but to agree. Thoughts went through my head that this could be a planned hit, but I had confidence that he was a good man because he had made such a large donation for the sake of oppressed children. My mind was made up. I would seek help outside my turf. When Maureen heard of my decision, she insisted that she go with me. I told her that if I got bumped off there would be no one to care for the children. She said she would go in another car or by herself if necessary but she wouldn't allow me to go alone.

So, on a specific night, we went to the restaurant to see Gus. As we walked in, he was standing at a bar in the front of the establishment. I introduced Maureen and myself and he coldly told me he wouldn't talk to me until we had dinner. He had a waitress escort us to a table in the back of the restaurant. The tables were covered with red and white checkered cloths like the ones in gangster movies, and the background was filled with opera music. We felt out of place and we didn't have money to spare for dinner. Therefore, we ordered spaghetti, which was the cheapest item on the menu.

While we were waiting for our food, we whispered our concerns to each other. The patrons in the restaurant were obviously regulars. They were friendly with the staff and many of them spoke Italian as they ordered their meals. I told Maureen to pray. We held hands under the table and told each other of our love.

The waitress arrived at our table with pasta and a large steak for each of us. I reminded her that we ordered spaghetti but she said that Gus instructed her to give us each a T-bone steak. We honestly felt that this may very well be our last meal. I suggested to Maureen that we enjoy the dinner but I felt that more than my gastric juices were about to flow. It was prime steak and I had no problem eating it, but Maureen couldn't finish hers. It was at that time that we were treated to coffee and cake.

When we finished, Gus approached our table. He asked if we enjoyed our meal. We thanked him, raved about the food, and he snapped his fingers. Immediately we were moved to an oval conference table with well-dressed people awaiting our company. Gus introduced us to them. The key person closest to us near the head of the table was a man named Hank with his wife. We were told that he was the managing editor of the local newspaper. There was also a councilman from Hillsdale, whose name I forget. Another person at that table was the Speaker of the House for the State of New Jersey. All the others were prominent people and very interested in what we had to say. Immediately, Maureen and I felt that they might be able to get that contract off our back and expedite care and concern for these children. There was no doubt in my mind that they also had the influence necessary to accomplish all of this and in record time.

We were then invited to present our case as Gus said he had other business to contend with. He wanted us to tell our story to his friends. He did all of this like he was playing the part of the "Godfather." He then left us. Maureen and I answered all their questions and they were obviously concerned for these innocent children.

Gus returned and said to Hank, "Are they alright?" He said absolutely.

Then Gus turned to us and asked how much money we needed. We told him we didn't want money and reiterated our needs. Concerning the contract he said, "Hold on." He then went to make a phone call.

While he was gone, I was in the mood to celebrate potential good news with these wonderful people and I bought them all a drink. I charged the drinks on my visa card not knowing how I'd ever pay for them. The receipt was put in front of me at the table.

Gus returned and told me nobody would bother my family or me. It was still unclear why we would have been given a death sentence but now that there was no contract on us we could again live our lives in peace instead of pieces.

He then looked down and noticed the receipt for the drinks. He said "What's this?" I told him I treated everyone a drink while he was gone.

He picked up the receipt and in his gruff voice said, "No one buys Gus' friends drinks." He then proceeded to rip it up.

Then he went around the table and asked his friends to volunteer to take the children from their placement in the Jersey City Medical Center and bring them to their homes temporarily until adequate care could be arranged for them. Almost all of them volunteered to take one or more children. Maureen and I couldn't believe our ears. Furthermore, how would he arrange for such placements to be made with the bureaucracy he'd be faced with? We hinted that he might have difficulty, but this met with many chuckles from his knights and ladies of the round table.

So far we were on a roll. We had one other request that we had no intention of mentioning but we simultaneously realized we must seize the moment.

We explained that we had a foster child living with us and we loved him and wanted to adopt him. However, his mother was very familiar with the laws of the State concerning adoption and would send him a $2.00 gift at Christmas. This was her only contact with him for the entire year and it made him ineligible for adoption. We needed a law passed that would change this stupid rule, which protected the mother's rights while the rights of the child were completely ignored.

There were no questions of us concerning this matter.

Gus pointed at the councilman from Hillsdale and instructed him to write a new law before he went to bed that night and give it to the Speaker of the House in the morning. He looked at him eyeball to eyeball and said he'd give him a month to pass it into law; and so he did.

Maureen and I bid all the ladies and gentlemen a fond adieu and got the hell out of there. Need I tell you that the fresh air never felt better and the grace of God and His Blessed Mother felt tangible and real. We were in absolute awe!

A week later, the local newspapers informed us that Mayor Whalen and his aide Gallagher were arrested for confiscating funds allocated to the Jersey City Medical Center to care for thirty-six children. Mysteriously, we were unable to account for one of the children but hopefully this was another DYFS error.

Not too long after that, the law was passed and our friends referred to it as the Niland Law. We were contacted by the court system shortly afterwards and were told to escort our son to the Hackensack Courthouse to finalize the adoption. A real gentleman lawyer named, Thomas Mahr, volunteered to be there on a pro bono basis. Tom served with us for fifteen years on the Juvenile Conference Committee in Paramus and his reputation for his concern for children was unsurpassed. He is one of my heroes in life.

As we entered the courthouse that day, we observed that there was a tremendous crowd of people. We felt that we would be there for hours. None of us liked waiting, especially in the cold environment of wood paneled walls and cold wooden benches.

At that time, a judge entered our area and asked to speak to Mr. and Mrs. Niland. Maureen was as surprised as I was. We spoke up and he informed us that we would be going first. Were it not for us, nobody else would have been there that day. All of the others were also going through adoption proceedings. We felt true joy in knowing that our efforts brought so much happiness to so many people.

Al Smith, our friend, had given my son a Gold Cross pen as a confirmation gift. We brought it with us for this special occasion. Judge Galda was presiding. He was the ex-mayor of Paramus and he was the first to sign the papers, then the rest of us signed on our dotted lines. Then I returned the pen to my son and we took him out to dinner for a celebration only the three of us could understand and appreciate. This was the culmination of many years of trying to finalize the adoption of a son that was sent to us as a gift from God. Our prayers were answered. This was a trying time for us but it sure had a happy ending.

As soon as we got home, we celebrated as a family. We had taken in Mary Ann when she was seven and we assumed she also wanted to be adopted

Her case was a sad one. She had been abused by both her mother and father and was considered one of the most difficult cases in Bergen County. When she came to live with us, she would hide food in her room and steal odds and ends from the household. She had trouble adjusting socially as well. She was in seven schools in the year she came to live with us and not surprisingly, her case workers never called to check up on how she was doing.

We gave her plenty of love and she found solace in the friendship offered by our neighbor, Debbie Lewis, who lived across the street. Debbie was the same age and introduced her into her circle of friends. Debbie was indeed a true Good Samaritan.

Mary Ann was one of five children. At one time it was important for her to stay in touch with each of them but after an initial exchange of photos, a couple of letters and a few phone calls her interest waned.

Because we had many boys, she was treated somewhat special because she was the only girl that was considered permanently placed with us. We treated her in every way as our own daughter.

When the announcement was made that our son's adoption was completed I said to her, "Hopefully you'll be next." She said she didn't want to be adopted. I told her to feel free to tell me if she ever changed her mind, but she never did.

After she was with us for many years, we received a call from the sheriff's office. He knew us personally. Maureen and I were members of The Police Chief's Organization of Bergen County. Although, I couldn't attend their meetings, Maureen was a regular. We had volunteered to be a Crisis Home for Children in need. The Sheriff informed us that they found Mary Ann's father dead in a flophouse and wanted to know if she would like to go through his things. He recommended that she didn't but was obligated to offer her the option.

Mary Ann elected to do it and I accompanied her as she went through his belongings. She was only interested in his personal belongings, not his funeral arrangements. She didn't want anything to do with him. He was cruel to her when he was alive and she didn't want to bother with him in death.

In her search she found a few photographs of her and her siblings. This seemed to satisfy her but she cried for weeks.

About a month later, the Sheriff called again. He said, I don't know how to tell you this but it is now believed that the dead man was apparently a boy friend of the mother, but not Mary Ann's father. The mother was presumed dead.

I told Mary Ann and she cried for another few weeks in intervals. It bewildered me that anyone could be so cruel and uncaring for their children. How could the mental scars ever leave her? We had no answer. All we could do is give her love and treat her like our daughter and a member of the family, which we did.

Maureen was especially good to her. As well as being her confidant, she catered to her and bought her special dresses. She was the daughter we never had.

Because she had such a tough life, I made it a point to pay her tuition at Bergen Community College. Unfortunately, she hung around with her friends during school hours and deceived me. Needless to say, the funding stopped.

10

DOESN'T ANYONE CARE?

We grew in faith as a family and we became very active in our church. Maureen became casual friends with one of the parishioners, Mary Lou Hawkins and knew that she and her husband were having difficulties. He used to drink heavily and with five children she became stressed at times. However, despite all her difficulties, she loved her children and was in every respect a model mother.

One evening, she was doing the wash and started to go downstairs in her house. She apparently missed a step and fell. The way she landed was unfortunate and her neck was broken. The police and ambulance were called but it was too late. Her body was viewed at Vander Platt's Funeral Home in Paramus. As funeral directors, their name is unsurpassed in our town. They are truly Christian soldiers and leaders in the community. They responded with special concerns for the needs of Mary Lou's five children but all that these siblings understood was that mother was dead and they would never see her walk the face of the earth again.

Maureen and I went to the wake. The five children were sitting on two upholstered benches as parishioners and friends piled in. We were sitting near the children, doing our best not to show any emotion that would upset them further. We tried not to convey our sadness over the occasion because they had enough of their own tears to contend with. Friends of the family, one by one, said a prayer as they knelt at the casket. They then filed past the children, reaching down to grasp their small hands. One by one, they uttered, "I'm so sorry." No doubt they were sorry but none of them asked what they could do to alleviate the children's pain. We said a prayer, just like the others, but as we held each of their hands, we simultaneously said we'd help them stay together as a family.

Their immediate family made an appearance to express their concern or more accurately put, just "showed up." It was very disconcerting.

Starting with the oldest, Nancy was 17, Howard, 14, Lauren, 12, Ellen, 10, and Steve about eight. All the children had blonde hair and blue eyes except for Ellen; she had red hair and was the one that closely resembled their mother. Also, all of the children were extremely bright and excelled in school without trying that hard scholastically.

Maureen and I met with family members. Their grandfather was the only one that was really concerned for them but his age prevented him from taking them into his personal care. He was willing but his body wasn't able.

For a short time, they were under their father's care. The grapevine told us that the kids were roaming the streets at night and weren't under any supervision. One night Nancy came to our house and apprised us of their situation. We went down to the house, which was a beautiful looking bi-level located near the Ridgewood Country Club Golf Course. Their father wasn't to be found. Although he was an electrician by trade, many of the lights didn't work and the kitchen was in total disarray. There was hardly any food in the refrigerator and there was a musty smell throughout the house. Although Nancy tried to maintain order, the job was insurmountable for a teenager. There was more than one problem stemming from the total disregard of their father. The facing on the cabinets popped off in many areas due to dampness, lack of maintenance, and lack of heat. The furnace wasn't working properly and their old man was out on a date with a very reputable person who never made it a point to realize the dilemma that these creatures of God were facing. It was difficult for me to comprehend how the pressure of my hand left a deep impression on the kitchen wall because of the dampness. Overall, the house was unkempt and the younger children were obviously not bathed.

Maureen tipped off the young lady that the father was dating. She was an intelligent woman who felt duped by her stupidity and after a tete-à-tete with him, discontinued their relationship.

The father's name was Howard, Sr. and was another maggot I encountered in my life. He had a silver tongue and referred to everyone by his or her first name. It was if he was a member of their family. He was totally consumed with himself and everyone else in his life played second fiddle. If you weren't aware of his family situation, you would swear that he was a model father while in fact; he was a poor provider, a bad listener, and a schemer of the worst sort.

If you believed him, he could account for every negative conclusion you might have drawn from your observations. He was like a politician whose hand was caught in the cookie jar.

We contacted their grandfather who had been a judge, and he instructed us to keep him informed if we discovered problems that his grandchildren were enduring. He promised decisive action.

Eventually, we were summoned to court and a judge held a hearing. It was determined that Howard, Sr. was not providing properly for the children and I can still hear the gavel accompanied with an echoing voice, "I award custody of the five children to Mr. and Mrs. Niland."

My heart was filled with mixed emotion. It was a victory for the children but an overwhelming albatross for Maureen and me. We had informed their grandfather that we would be willing to take them as an answer to their short term need and we would seek out homes nearby where the children would be loved and properly cared for. Financially, we couldn't handle this burden so they were put under the auspices of the Division of Youth and Family Services. We had to scurry to make ready sleeping arrangements and we analyzed our living situation.

We had our sons Denis, Brian and John. There was also Richie and Jimmy; two brothers we gave temporary homes to, Mary Ann, who was a permanent resident, and Lillian, who spent weekends with us. There were a couple other kids staying with us but we didn't tell the State or we would have been inundated with an army of incompetent social workers complaining about their caseloads. After all, why tell them, they didn't ask.

At the time, I believe we had fourteen children. This was the most we ever had at one time. We knew we had many children but we didn't count them. However, if one of them was missing, we knew about it in seconds because a missing child leaves a tremendous void and that has to be addressed immediately.

In those days our dog Princess had to be put down. She was as perfect a pet that anyone could hope to have. The children were depressed after losing their close friend and I agreed to take them dog hunting, knowing well that they would never mutually agree on the same dog. We went to a kennel near Trenton and they all fooled me and agreed on one dog, which was named, "Snoopy." I took him to a Vet for his shots and was told the dog was almost all wolf. I found this absurd. However, Snoopy grew up to be vicious and got along with only a handful of people. Whenever another child entered into our house, I'd have to extend a handful of peanuts and then give a handful to the child. Their hand would then be extended several times until Snoopy grunted. This meant the child could stay but not necessarily remain as a friend. We also had a stupid dog, a Collie, named Shawn. He lacked many attributes.

One night, when we had fourteen children, Maureen and I were having a cup of tea in the kitchen. Many of the children were rapping up their assignments, which were on a rotating schedule. One of the teenage boys came back from walking the dogs and was removing the leashes from their necks; all this while Snoopy was threatening him. He uttered the following, "Thank God I don't have to walk Snoopy for another two weeks." At that time we laughed and realized for the first time that we had fourteen children under the same roof.

Maureen and I spoke to our neighbors, the "Froms." They had raised three daughters. One was married and another was in college. The younger one was still going to school locally. We asked them if they could take in young Howard. They met him and agreed to do so. Howard Jr. was able to help Joe From with his gardening, do shopping and learned from Joe how to repair things and most importantly how to deal with people. Jeanne was a wonderful cook and satisfied young Howard's palette at every meal she served. Frequently, Howard would come home from school and go directly to our house where he would socialize with his brothers and sisters.

Nancy was with us a relatively short time before she went to the University of Nevada. She was a brilliant and beautiful girl with a bright future. It was a difficult decision she made. She was the first to put miles between herself and her family. However, she was too young to accept the responsibility of four siblings. Steve was the youngest and I think he missed her the most.

Ellen was a good friend of the LaMothe Family. Their daughter and Ellen were close buddies. Maureen asked the family, who lived five minutes away if they would take in Ellen as a foster child and they said yes.

Lauren was the last to be placed. She was already in trouble with her circle of the wrong friends. She had a big heart but made big mistakes. Maureen convinced the Grothues Family to take her in as a foster child. They agreed. However, Lauren, after six months or so told me she couldn't live there any longer. I asked her why and she told me that there is nothing but love in that house and it's driving her nuts. I told her that I couldn't believe my ears. This family was close friends of ours and had high hopes for her. I told Lauren that if she decided to leave this family, she would be placed by the State and this was not good. Maureen and I gave her the opportunity she needed. If she didn't want to accept it; she would have to pay the price. She opted to pay the price and she did.

Steve was the youngest of the five and Maureen and I decided that we'd keep him. It was a delight raising him as my son. He loved sports, especially baseball. I encouraged him as much as I could to play Little League. His coach, Vic Moreno, knew about his situation and spent extra time with him. Steve was a good ball player and liked short stop and second base when he played.

At the beginning of one of the seasons, I went to register him and pay the fee that was due. I was told that he was already registered and paid for. I told the volunteer that this couldn't be so but he insisted. I asked him, who paid and registered him? He referred to the records and said, "Mr. Moreno." I said to myself, this is what coaching is all about. Naturally, I thanked Vic. He said he wanted to be sure that Steve wasn't deprived of playing ball. However, he reminded me that Steven had to wear cleats but objected to this rule. I told him I was aware of the rules and just bought him a new pair.

When I took Steve to his first game that year, he refused to wear his cleats. He said he wouldn't under any circumstances. I told him the rules were strict. If he didn't abide by the rules, he couldn't play. He said he would play whether I liked it or not. I hid his uniform and his sneakers and cleats and drove all the other boys to their game. Then I drove Steve home and turned on the Yankee game. I told him that since he was going to be a spectator for the rest of his life, he might as well get used to it. Shortly after the first inning, he came to his senses. We got to his game in the third inning. He was clad in cleats and went three for four.

Steve enjoyed basketball as well. I remember Maureen buying him a new pair of jeans that he took to a game in the school gym. His friend's father arrived as they were playing. He was boozed up and demanded that his son leave immediately. The father grabbed Steve's pants and said, "Put these on." The kid was embarrassed. He said the pants weren't his. The response was, "Don't give me that crap, I said put them on." When Steve came home with the old pair of pants, with holes in them; Maureen asked what happened. When I heard of this, I told Steve to tell his friend to arrange for a pants switch but he said his father, who worked for the Sheriff's Office wouldn't hear of it. I informed Steve to tell his friend to inform his father that I have no other option but to go to his house and beat the shit out of his father. Well, he told his father and the poor kid brought Steve's pants to school for him the next day. This was the case of "The Maggot in the Uniform of the Law."

Bad luck to him!

Before Ellen was placed with the LeMothe's she went to the eye doctor for a new prescription. She was then fitted for frames, for which the State paid. The next day, she came home from school crying. Her classmates said she was wearing "institutional frames." Children can be so cruel. Maureen and I went out that night and got her different and stylish frames. Naturally, the State wouldn't pay the difference.

I'd be remiss, if I didn't tell you what became of the five children. Nancy gained scholarship after scholarship and graduated from the University of Nevada. She called us several times but only visited us once or twice. She became a Pediatrician and a Child Psychologist on the west coast. Howard went into the Air Force and attended military school in Monterey where he learned Korean. He now has a computer company in Wisconsin. Rather than thanking the Froms, he felt they were obligated to give him money for his business. When they refused, he refused to talk to them again. He then borrowed money from Nancy, which he lost, and I believe they're not on speaking terms. Lauren has been messed up ever since. I do hope that she puts it all together some day. She has a warm heart and was the victim of a bad break in her life. Ellen is gainfully employed out West and seems to be enjoying life. I don't hear from her. Steve is a schoolteacher in Nevada. He's thinking about coming East once again. He married a wonderful girl, Ashley. They have three wonderful children and they are busy improving their overall education, which will enable them to live more comfortably in the future. They have their own house and Steve enjoys playing catch with his boys. He shows them the same love he received from me. We talk on the phone a couple times a week.

In the midst of all this turmoil, DYFS gave us a certificate to frame and hang on the wall. It proclaimed that we were "Foster Parents of the Year." How stupid, how could we hang such a certificate and make a kid living with us feel at home. It merely proclaimed to the world that they were second-class citizens.

I prayed that I would become a better father to all the children. I loved them but felt I should do more to provide for them. All I knew was that Maureen and I were truly doing our very best.

Shopping was a classic. I'd bring a station wagon full of kids and leave the others at home. We had a little game that we played. We'd enter the store with the smallest leading the pack. At the command, three of them would peel off and grab carts. We'd then invade the aisles. Shoppers looked at us in total disbelief. As planned one of the kids would touch a piece of fruit and I pretended to whack him in the head, while slapping my chest. He'd respond by faking the hit. Old ladies would seek someone in authority to put a halt to my abuse. We repeated our shenanigans many times but managed to fill three baskets in twenty minutes. The whole shopping trip would be a half-hour door to door.

To pay those bills, I would always take advantage of the interest-free offers from banks with their credit cards. This was a system I mastered.

The Hawkins children were loveable, and I wish I could have taken all of them myself but we did afford them the opportunity to stay together as a family. Part of the problem was that the father was such a conniver. He'd call me from time to time saying he needed one of the kids' social security numbers. I'd give him the wrong number and get him out of my hair for another six months, but he was like a bad nickel; you couldn't get rid of him.

My neighbors were great to the children. Frieda Girolamo's husband Peter died at a young age and left her with three children. She did a great job raising them while at the same time extending love and concern for all the kids at the Nilands. The Lewis Family had three daughters. They were groundbreakers for all the children that came to stay with us. They'd introduce our children to new friends, help them with school and share their love and concern. John and Dot Lewis were the closest friends we ever had. We cried years later when they moved to South Jersey and eventually to California. They threw the greatest parties. Sometimes, the celebrations went on for days. Their New Year's Eve parties were known in the tri-state area. John was fun and loved his beer. He was a Colonel in the Air Force Reserves and when he moved to California, he went into panic mode when he realized that they didn't sell his favorite beer. This was a crisis! This was his housewarming party. Just then, the roar of two helicopters passed over and with absolute precision dropped keg after keg in his back yard. Naturally, each keg bore the brand name of his favorite beer. This house warming gift was more than a pleasant surprise for John. The Rosenbergs took in a boy as a foster son but it didn't work out. Later, they took in another and they eventually adopted him. They had two other sons. Mr. Rosenberg or "Richie" as we called him, loved German Shepherds but his wife objected over the thought of his getting one. His hobby of flying model airplanes was too much for her already. However, his marriage was in jeopardy when he brought home a stupid German Shepherd named Bruce. He frequently went through the screen door and ran for blocks. He also had a terrible habit of taking bites out of the couch in the living room.

Then there was Rudy and Adele. Rudy owned a dental lab and went to work early each day. He always invited me to ride with him if I had to go in early. In those days, I'd have to be in to give weather reports to the news media on bad days. One time we were expecting a storm and I arranged to accompany him but I canceled when the forecast changed for the better. Therefore, Rudy went in to work early by himself. He used to park his car on the roof of the Port Authority Bus Terminal. On that morning when he exited his car, he was mugged. After the four thugs took all his money, wallet, and credit cards they battered him some more and threw him into the trunk of his Cadillac. They then went on a wild ride on the New York Thruway when a toll collector noticed a couple of fingers, protruding from the rear of the vehicle, desperately trying to attract attention. Somehow, Rudy managed to unlock the trunk. The toll collector contacted the State Troopers and they chased the car at high speeds. The felons then pulled over and ran into the woods where there was a shoot out. Thank God, Rudy was alive. That night, he knocked on my door to inquire the time of the Masses at church. He promised God that he'd go to church every Sunday if he escaped alive from the trunk. At that time, I found out that the culprits called his home and demanded ransom. Furthermore, I was an early suspect on the FBI's list because I had canceled going in with him. However, Adele vouched for me.

At this juncture, knowing Rudy was safe, I found it humorous to know that Rudy felt he made a deal with God when he was in the trunk. Clearly, I understood why there are no atheists in foxholes. Last I heard, they were retired in Las Vegas.

11

ORDINATION

One evening, a great priest, Father Chester Zega, a personal friend, came to visit Maureen and me. He was the kind of guy that was special as a member of the clergy. I knew him well because he was the moderator of the Holy Name Society and I was an active member. He wanted to know his parishioners personally. Furthermore, the pastor, Father Coyle and Father Zega weren't on speaking terms. No one really knew the history as to why; but the regular churchgoers were aware that Father Coyle was a guzzler of good scotch and it reflected on him negatively and he didn't get along with people. I guess it was a breath of fresh air visiting the congregation at large for Father Zega. He made it a point to visit everyone he could. He'd dress casually but was rendered the greatest of respect because he was a true Christian and friend.

One of my children answered the door for him. As he passed the bathroom on the main floor, he asked if smoke should be coming from the bathroom. After greeting him, he took a seat in the kitchen and I went off to investigate the smoke he allegedly observed.

When I opened the bathroom door fully (it had been slightly ajar), I observed flames as well. I called out to Maureen and she called the fire department. The clothes dryer from Sears was the culprit, it was on fire. I don't think Sears ever overcame the likelihood of lint fires in this appliance. This happened in the early seventies when Sears was losing their dominance in the appliance market because they refused to listen to their customers. It was here that they crossed that imaginary line with me and lost me as a customer. Bad luck to them!

The fire engines responded quickly and extinguished the flames. However, as the first firefighter entered the house, Snoopy went into the attack mode and pulled the boot off of him and ripped it apart. Once he was collared, the dryer was put at the curb and the house was vented. Finally, when the firefighters left, we sat down to talk.

Father Zega explained that he wanted to discuss with me the possibility of my becoming a Deacon in the Catholic Church. I had no idea what he was talking about. He explained that a Deacon goes through a period of training and eventually can perform many of the Rites, normally reserved at the time for priests. He said that the Order of Deacons had been revived by Vatican II's decision. Deacons will be able to read the Gospel, distribute Holy Communion, preach, baptize, and officiate at funerals and weddings. They would not be able to anoint the sick or hear confessions. Anointing and Penitential Rites involve the forgiveness of sins and only priests can perform these acts. This special gift is given to them at their ordination. He said the Deaconate was a ministry being offered to single men who would not be able to marry after ordination and to married men who would not be able to marry if their wife died, unless they received special dispensation. He said that a friend of mine, Bill Joyce, had already expressed an interest in going through the program. It would involve several years of training at a site decided upon by the Archdiocese. He then asked if I would be interested. I told him he wouldn't get an answer from me that night. I knew that a symbol of the Holy Spirit was tongues of fire, and I certainly saw plenty of fire that evening, but the possibility of going through with this would have to be discussed with Maureen in great detail and also with the children. I told him that I was initially interested but I had a lot to sleep on. He said he understood. He laughed over my comment regarding the tongues of fire and we recalled the homily he gave one day on the Holy Spirit. There had been a bird that managed to enter the church. When he announced that he was going to talk about the Holy Spirit, the bird landed on the ambo as he began to preach. His initial comment was, "I couldn't have planned this better." We laughed, enjoyed a beer and called it a night.

Maureen and I knew that such a program would be a blessing for our family. We knew that a great deal of time together would be sacrificed and it would mean more commuting costs. This was a volunteer ministry, which meant no pay. We didn't know if we could bear the brunt of it. After much discussion, we realized that it was something for a husband and wife to share. We already had a ministry and that was being involved with children. We knew that we could help children more with this wonderful blessing, which the church reinstalled after more than a thousand years. We agreed that we would call the family together and if anyone was against it, the idea would fizzle. We had our get together and the whole family agreed that it was the way to go. They realized that it would mean less quality time together but they looked forward to my ordination. There are seven sacraments in the Catholic Church. Despite what I was told by the nuns in grammar school that you couldn't receive all of them, they were wrong.

First, I had to go through an investigative process after I announced my interest. A priest, Father Papara came to my house to check my family out. On that night, we had four kids with problems and we were trying to help them.

One problem was Nancy Hawkins who brought her guitar and wanted to talk about the chaos in her family. Because she was somewhat of a regular, we sent her to the dining room to play music while we tried to handle the other situations. One child was with me, another with Maureen and the third with my buddy, Father Jim Garvie who spent most of his evenings with us rather than sit in the rectory and witness the wall of silence which separated Father Coyle and Father Zega. Upon the arrival of Father Papara, we dispatched him to sit with Nancy. He left that night inspired and focused his homily the next day on his visit to our home. My children interacted with him and he felt he provided consoling words for Nancy. He said he witnessed the working of the Holy Spirit like never before. Well, I was encouraged by his words and eventually I was enrolled in the second Deaconate Class of the Archdiocese of Newark.

It was required that a candidate attend two classes a week. The classes were held in Saint Joseph's Church in a ghetto area of Newark. The church had only four parishioners and was in dire straits. We couldn't stand in certain parts of the building because the floors were too weak to hold our weight. If we missed a class, it was mandatory that we watch it on the TV taped version, which was the remedy if someone couldn't make it.

The Director of the program was a genius named Monsignor McGuiness. The size of the class was overwhelming and many of the candidates were cut within the first six months. While sitting with many of them during discussions, one could realize that they could be potential problems. All cuts were made with dignity and respect. The teachers were from Seton Hall University. They were knowledgeable and projected their love for God as they taught. They were so exceptional that their instructions stimulated a special interest for Bill Joyce and me as we commuted to Newark together. Bill is probably the smartest guy that I have ever known. He was slightly younger than me and had projected that I would be ordained a year and a half sooner than him. This didn't make sense but I guess someone had to determine age requirements. One of the problems with our schooling was stolen video equipment, but the Deacons invited the teenage thieves into the church and taught them plumbing and carpentry; they eventually became watchdogs at the church. Saint Joseph's Church had practically no heat and we kept our coats on in the winter. In the summer, we missed the air conditioning but welcomed the sacrifice in knowing that we were able to accommodate the local Deacons who couldn't afford to travel from other Archdiocesan counties. Traveling to the ghetto invoked the spirit we shared.

It was sad seeing one of the priests, a Father Caprio, who had been instrumental in the formation of the program leave the priesthood. It was also much of a surprise when the historian of the Archdiocese, Monsignor Beck, also left. He taught us Church History and then flew the coop. It was difficult to accept the fact that this Monsignor elected to vacate his office. This was a time of change for the priesthood. Many of the young priests questioned their vocations and disputed the fact that priests couldn't marry. Somewhere along the line, commitment was thrown out the window. However, I saw the value in quality for those that stayed and remained true to their ordination. Maybe I still had that Marine Corps Sergeant in me along with the recruitment motto, "We're looking for a few good men."

We had more than a few good men teaching us. Father Turro, an author of several books, was an inspiration. He used to deliver his classes standing in his black raincoat. He was totally involved in his teaching. I invited him to my home for dinner but he said he would never be able to make it. He really didn't socialize with anyone. It was all "God" business with him. Once he did surprise me and showed up at my home. That night, we had one of our favorite visitors, Laurie, who was a young girl with real problems. During our discussion that night, he reached into his wallet to give me a phone number. He called our attention to the wallet and said a friend gave it to him. It was genuine leather and hand stitched. He said his friend must have spent a great deal of money for it. Laurie saw the wallet and spoke up saying, "I got the same one in Englishtown for a buck fifty." Needless to say, we had a great laugh.

Father Turro had the reputation of giving one-minute homilies that sent you out of the pew discussing what he had said for the entire day. He was extremely likable and somewhat unpredictable. Once he gave a class on Saint Paul. He had us think about his comments and disappeared. The next week, I asked him if he had to leave early for some reason because I was anxious to hear what else he had to say on the subject. He said, "That's all there was to say." He was different in a wonderful way.

Then there was Father Frank McNulty. He was the Spiritual Director for Priests in the Archdiocese. He was called upon by his fellow priests to represent them when Pope John Paul II came to New Jersey at Giant Stadium. Because everyone is concerned about giving the congregation a good homily, he left us with this thought: Every day, we witness a homily; but we will miss it if we aren't focused in our ministry. I found this to be true.

Father Philip Morris was again beautifully different. He used to leave us with things to think about. I can remember once he said life is merely the interruption of non-existence. What a great discussion we had on this thought. Twenty years later, I officiated at a wedding in his parish. He welcomed me in a most cordial manner. While we awaited the arrival of the bride, I mentioned his quote. He said it sounded familiar and was tickled when he heard that it came from his lips so many years ago.

There was a Monsignor Murray who conned me into assisting him, to a minor degree, in promoting an Archbishop's Appeal because the Archdiocese was in hock up to its eyeballs. He told us that this would be a one-time appeal. The next year he was back again. The claim was that no one ever made such a statement. Naturally, it has been ongoing since. I don't contribute to this appeal because of several reasons. First, I was lied to. Second, I was told that there would be money that would go to the Deaconate. That promise was abandoned. I realize that there are legitimate bills to be paid but this method of operating a charity resembles, "Three Card Monty," which is played on the street of most cities and lures unsuspecting tourists.

One night there was an elderly priest who I don't believe recognized the reason for the Deaconate. As we exited the building from classes, he attempted to hand me his car keys with the instruction to get his vehicle so he wouldn't get wet. Bad luck to him! Poor guy didn't even have an umbrella!

There were so many great men who gave their lives for God. They did a fantastic job teaching us. Father Gusmer taught us how to perform religious rites. He was discussing full immersion experiences at baptismal fonts when he started to explain that once an infant defecated in the water but he wanted to keep his instruction sophisticated and wanted to avoid using guttural language. He struggled for the right words, hemming and hawing for almost thirty seconds when he proclaimed that the baby tainted the font. Naturally, we laughed.

When we were about to graduate, we were surveyed to determine what was especially meaningful in our training. All of us raved about the dedication, sincerity and competence of the teaching staff. We also felt that the spirit of Saint Joseph's Church was instrumental in bringing different ethnic groups together in praise to the Lord. Also, we shared our ministries and helped each other out. We all felt that Saint Josephs must be a part of the program. Each of us, instead of sheepskin, got a piece of one of the pews when we graduated from the program. Written on the wood from the pew was stated that we had completed the program. Saint Josephs was then sold.

On December 12, 1976, Archbishop Gerrity ordained me to the order of Deacon in the Catholic Church; he was a man all of us respected.

On that day, my family filled a whole pew at Sacred Heart Cathedral in Newark. They purchased my vestments. They put them on me and embraced me with loving arms. All of them had earned part of my ordination and it was time for a victory party for all of them. We held that celebration in the school hall and many parishioners were invited. Unfortunately, we couldn't accommodate everyone.

Prior to that day of Ordination, Bill and I became Ministers of the Word, which meant we could profess the Gospel at Mass, and Ministers of the Eucharist, meaning we could distribute Holy Communion.

It was sad to observe so many people going to receive Communion from priests rather than from a Deacon. Many felt our hands were not consecrated and we were unworthy. So the Deacons had to assume a role of humility. As we know, we have many lay people assisting with the distribution of the Holy Eucharist today. They came around, but we found that people do not respond well to change when it involves religion.

Some priests like Fathers Garvie and Father Zega welcomed me into the fold but others built a wall of indifference. Young priests were more tolerant of our roles in the Church than many of the older priests who were more set in their ways.

It was also a great day when Bill Joyce was ordained. He's a role model and never really made a commotion about the delay in his Ordination. He and his wife and family have accompanied me in over thirty years of ministry at Annunciation in Paramus. Judy and Bill have been instrumental in the success of the Marriage Encounter Program in the Archdiocese. Judy was the unfortunate one in a million who got the swine flu and almost died from it. She needs our prayers.

The effect of being a Deacon has had a profound effect on my children. It is certainly a factor in making them different from their peers. They are not afraid to be that person to step forward to present a different idea. They have reached out and touched others in a special way and are frequently the volunteers to give help to the poor and oppressed.

For a brief time after being ordained a Deacon, I was invited to serve on the Board of Directors for the Catholic Youth Organization. I assisted them with the formation of job descriptions and establishing an Evaluation System to determine a method to provide them with a fair salary. After a couple years, I resigned my position. It wasn't my bag; too many meetings, obstacles to accomplish goals, and opinions that weren't thought out and were submitted spontaneously at the last minute at meetings. Also, they thought "manual labor" was a Mexican.

This involvement also took me away from my family. My ministry belonged in my home. It was there where the action was.

If it wasn't for being a Deacon, I don't think Maureen and I would have been involved with helping the Vietnam Boat People. This was a topic that was close to our hearts. We felt strongly that our country should support them and offer help; especially after we abandoned them after the war.

Their need for help fulfilled the question I asked one of the nuns that taught me in grammar school. She was teaching us the various acts of charity. One of them in the old "Baltimore Catechism" was to "Harbor the harbor less." I asked her what this meant. She obviously didn't know. She said "Just memorize all of them."

The peak of these people's turmoil was in the summer following the end of the war. Maureen's birthday was just around the corner and a multimillionaire contacted her to offer assistance. He said he owned a large yacht and was willing to use it if it could be helpful in our plight. She worked it out that we could sell tickets for a cruise around Manhattan for $20.00. She didn't want birthday presents. She wanted to help these poor people. We were doing our best to promote this project and we had begun to make real headway.

One night, we were having dinner. We had a strict rule that no one could receive any phone calls at the dinner table. We treasured our coming together to share thoughts, ideas and dreams. We emphasized the importance of being positive with each other and never argue. Well, wouldn't you know it, that night the phone rang. The child closest to the phone answered it and listened to the caller for a moment and then interrupted and said, "I'm sorry, we're having dinner. Could you please call back?" At the end of our meal I asked who the caller was. I was told it was Vice President Walter Mondale and he apologized for interrupting our dinner and he would call back and he did. He apologized once again and my wife told him about our project. He seemed very interested in it.

On July 4, we all convened near the Battery in New York City. The yacht couldn't dock because there were so many kids shooting fireworks at it. Finally, as the night became morning it was able to board passengers. The boat was filled with contributors, and they all enjoyed their cruise.

Another one of the special moments was the visit of Pope John Paul II to Giant Stadium in New Jersey. It was such a privilege to be invited to be a Deacon at the Mass. There was a torrential rainstorm that night and the alb I wore was so wet that it must have weighed ten pounds. I was called upon to distribute Holy Communion on the upper deck. The wind was blowing fiercely. The Communion Hosts were in a silver bowl covered with saran wrap. As I peeled back the plastic, the hosts swirled in the bowl. It became a methodical chore, but it was such an honor. When the Mass ended, I began the walk to my car. I walked on the field with hundreds of others. There was a lack of fulfillment in my heart because I never really got close to the Pope. Just as I was exiting from the main gate of the stadium, I was stopped in my tracks by the Secret Service. A limousine pulled up in front of me. There he was. I was at arm's length from the Pope. He smiled at me and I was in awe. This was one of the most priceless moments of my life.

Dinners were always special, and Maureen was a dynamic cook. Her specialty was Armenian food. However, she could also prepare traditional meals. One Thanksgiving, a great meal was planned. Unfortunately, I got called into work because of the inclement weather. I was on standby because I was guaranteed Christmas off. That Thanksgiving, Channel Eleven called and wanted to take TV pictures of our family during dinner. The idea of such a large family coming together to share prayers and a meal had appeal. That year, I missed a wonderful Thanksgiving meal but saw it on TV tape. That was the year I had a TV dinner for Thanksgiving.

12

PHIL AND PAUL

Around the Christmas season many people look to do some good, whether it's meant to ease their consciences or spread the love of Christ. In the mid seventies, Maureen and I formed a small group of parishioners to bring cheer to group homes in Newark. The plan was to visit the homes and determine what the residents wanted for Christmas. The homes were well run. There was a manager on duty around the clock. The two that I visited were Brownstones and had twelve residents each. All of them were mentally challenged. They were full of love and knew nothing about the competitive world they lived in. Their hearts were free from prejudice and they enjoyed the simple chores they were given in the group home. When we visited them, the most popular request for gifts included cigarettes and music. They weren't fussy about the brand of cigarette or the type of music. In any case, we took their names and request on our initial visit. The committee then went out and satisfied their simple wants. Nobody had a lavish request so the gifts were quite affordable.

About two weeks prior to Christmas, I dressed up in a Santa's outfit and all of us went to the two homes. We had a bell to attract attention and the residents shouted like little children that Santa had arrived. I had a bag of gifts with names on them. When each person's name was called, they reacted with glee. Most of them ripped off the gift-wrapping in their excitement. This was a great fun project. It was even a great success the first year we did it.

During Santa's initial visit the next year, one of the residents named Paul approached me and said he had to find someplace to live. He said that the people who ran the house told him that he was now able to go off on his own. I told him I would try to find him a place to live. After praying for help because we didn't know where to turn, we thought of Mount Saint Andrew's Villa. This was a home for elderly people. If they could provide him with room and board, he could work on the premises. Maureen and I spoke with the Director, Sister Clare Magellen. This nun was an angel! It was a mystery to me how they survived financially. She told me that she would welcome Paul, but that they only had a very small room available; it was certainly too small to provide much comfort. I agreed, the room was small but considering the situation, it was just right. Paul got his Christmas wish that year. It was a perfect arrangement. The nuns gave him guidance and provided him with a paycheck. He served meals in their dining room, landscaped, painted and performed chores if he was given specific instructions. Sometimes he screwed up, but don't we all?

Paul formed a close relationship with everyone at the Villa. He was very religious and found solace speaking to the nuns and Father Santora who was retired but said Mass each morning in their Chapel.

One day Paul came to me and said he had a problem. He had a look of dire concern on his face. He told me that his brother was told that he had to leave his home and needed a place to stay. He told me his brother's name was Phil and they were twins. It appears they were abandoned at birth. I told Paul that I would speak to Sister Clare once again.

Sister Clare initially thought I was kidding her. When she saw that I wasn't she said that she had no vacant rooms. The thought of sharing Paul's room was really out of the question because it was too small. I conveyed this information to Paul who insisted it was not too small, "He's my brother." That sounded familiar and I went back to Sister Clare who folded like a cheap camera. Both brothers got along well with everyone, but they needed supervision.

Because I helped them get situated, they felt obligated to do things for me. Despite the realization that it is Christ like to be friendly with them, you must realize that they can consume a good part of your life if you allow it. So, the solution is to say hello, be pleasant and move on. To explain this better, allow me to give you some examples of what I mean.

One spring, I was trying to solve my lawn problems. For once, I went overboard on grass seed. The bag was large and cost about seventy dollars. I put the bag on the driveway and retreated to the garage to get the spreader. Something distracted me but finally I got back to the business at hand. As I returned to the driveway, Phil and Paul were standing where I left the bag of grass. I asked them if they knew where the bag was. They told me, I was their friend and they took care of it. I asked them where they put the seed. Their answer was, "a little here and a little there." I got the idea. It was time to buy more grass.

Another time, Maureen went to Norton's Paint Store and had the paint guru, Mr. Norton, mix a small can of Colonial Blue for our shutters. I got a paint tarpaulin and put it under the window, opened the paint can, and put a clean brush next to it. Then I responded to a lengthy phone call. When I finished, I went outside and they were painting my house. I said, "Hold it!" but it was too late.

I then had to go back to Norton's and have them match my faded house paint and mix another can of Colonial Blue.

The two of them were tireless. Once they came running down the hill from the Villa waving two new snow shovels. There had just been a dusting of snow and they insisted on shoveling it for me. I told them that the temperatures were going to rise and everything would be melted in a couple hours. Still, they insisted. They started to shovel and within ten minutes their shovels broke. There's a screw that they should have used to fasten the handle to the shovel but they neglected to do it. I told them that Sears should have assembled them and I drove them back to Sears. I couldn't get a parking space at Paramus Park. We were in the peak of the busy Christmas shopping; so I parked in front of the store, waiting for them with the engine running. They came out a half hour later with the same shovels and said the man wouldn't help them. I grabbed the shovels and had them wait in the car. I charged down the aisle and the sales clerk knew I was pissed. In self-defense, he held up two replacement shovels. I grabbed them. Nothing else, not even a word was exchanged; just the shovels. Then we went back to my house. We had to go downstairs to the basement where I put the screws into the handle. We then went outside to finish the job, but the snow had melted.

Paul then asked if they could have some hot chocolate. Naturally, Maureen and I treated them. I didn't have dinner that night but went to sleep knowing that I survived yet another invasion from the two of them.

The nuns kept them on their premises most of the time but occasionally they went for a walk. They developed a habit of buying radio scanners. They monitored police and fire activities. They also used CB radios to communicate with each other.

Since two of my sons were cops, they liked it when they'd stop and say hello to them in their squad cars.

When Brian moved from his first house to his new one, he told me not to tell them where he now lived. They asked and I felt guilty not telling them but understood my son's reasoning. Then they saw my son Denis who gave them Brian's phone number. Brian's wife, Barbara, didn't know either of them until Paul called. When she answered, a voice on the other end said, "I know where you live." In a panic, Barbara slammed down the phone. Today, they look forward to seeing Barbara. She always greets them as special friends.

Phil and Paul received a letter from an anonymous source. Because they couldn't read, they brought it to me. It informed them that they had a brother. This was a challenge. It was in the pre-computer era and took many months and many letters before I made contact with their brother. It seems he was a missionary in South America and informed them that they had a sister, but I wasn't about to rise to that challenge.

I'll never forget when they received their Confirmation. I lost out on two suits for that occasion. When they arrived at my house for me to approve their garb, Phil was wearing muddy boots. Maureen told me I didn't need the spare pair of shoes I had in the closet. To torment me further, Maureen had me get two red ties and put knots in them. I survived that day too.

I remember one Easter Vigil when Paul stood up and told the congregation that his brother would undergo a heart operation that very evening. Everyone was concerned for him as he begged them to pray for his brother.

The next morning, Easter Sunday, I asked my sons to do me a special favor and dress in their police and fire uniforms and we'd visit Phil in the hospital. We went to Valley Hospital where volunteers manage the Information Desk. Some are well meaning and competent, but some are difficult to deal with. On that day, an elderly woman told me that Phil was discharged. I insisted that this couldn't be but she insisted that it was so. She said he left the hospital at 10:20 pm last night. I knew this was not true but getting the room number from this woman was impossible. My sons were forgiving. I called Paul all day but got no answer. I figured he was visiting his brother in the hospital and I eventually found out that was exactly where he was. I was able to contact him in the evening and went to visit him then.

When I got to the hospital, I proceeded to his room. As I arrived there, he was in the foyer and saw me. He said hello and lifted up his hospital gown and showed me where he had been cut by the surgeon. Needless to say, there were many onlookers or should I saw, "gawkers."

Sister Clare passed away and the number of nuns at the Villa declined. There was less supervision for the twins and they started to be present at church while all the Masses were being said on Sundays. They were very religious, and although their appearance might frighten someone who didn't know them, they were truly harmless. They made it a point to attend Mass with the Thompson family. Bob and his wife, Denise, are special people. They have a large and wonderful family. He even brings him to the adult softball games he plays. They have become favorite spectators on the softball fields.

When Mount Saint Andrew's Villa closed its doors, Father Bill worked things out with the State and Phil and Paul rented a house in New Milford. They are in one sense self-dependent, but in actuality, unable to budget for themselves and have special needs.

Father Bill, or should I say, Mr. Bill, left the priesthood and got married. Initially, he stayed in touch with them on a regular basis but not so much anymore.

It was such a meaningful experience working with the Sisters of Charity from Convent Station. Their dedication to their ministry of taking care of the elderly and handicapped is unsurpassed.

After my mother died, my father went to live with my brother Larry. That didn't work out and he eventually lived with Maureen and me. He sought a special peace at times and rented a room at the Villa. Whenever he'd be there for a few days, he'd call me and say, "Son, take me home." Again, when the kids got to be too much for him, he'd say, "Son, take me home." The commuting distance between the Villa and my house was one block. Sometimes he'd call when he'd run out of Scotch and I'd send him a refill with a couple of Twinkies. Upon the messenger's (one of the kids) arrival, he'd carefully put away the bottle and give them the Twinkies. One of the nuns walked in on him one night as he was having a nightcap. He wasn't the least bit startled. He invited her to have a drink with him and she did. My dad had an ulcer and had to be careful and so he was; he used to drink his Scotch with a little milk. These were special days for my dad. He used to enjoy watching the kids if Maureen had to go somewhere, but all his baby-sitting had to be for short periods. He'd get cranky but that was understandable. At times we had a lot of kids.

13

TRIALS, TRIBULATIONS AND ACCOMPLISHMENTS

On New Year's Eve, 1975, our Holy Name Society was planning a New Year's Eve Party. I was asked to make arrangements for a band. A friend of mine, Don Minard, played in a band part time. He was also a manager at the Auto Club. He said he didn't do gigs on New Year's Eve but his band did. I asked Dave Reuben, another employee at AAA if the band was available. He said, "Yes, for six hundred dollars." A contract also had to be signed. The Holy Name agreed to go along with the arrangements, but a month before the big date, they decided they didn't have enough people to make the dance a financial or social success. I reminded them of the contract I signed and the fact that I paid a $200 deposit. We all voted that I should negotiate with the band and do my best to get it for the cheapest price. I apprised Dave of the situation and asked him if the band members would give us a break because it was for the church. He said he'd ask the other members. He quickly got back to me and said they were unwilling to help. They wanted their six hundred dollars. I conveyed my difficult situation to Don Minard. He said he couldn't do anything about it but heard that the band members were booking other jobs for the big date. Based on this information, I played hardball. I told Dave that I wanted the band to go to the rectory at 9:00 p.m. on New Year's Eve and play Irish songs to Emily, the housekeeper. He objected but I told him, "If we pay, you play." Naturally, he was ticked, but bad luck to him. We gave them the deposit money as payment in full. They elected to give us a break after all.

Emily never got to hear the band but Father (Chet) Zega had a date with her every Wednesday. They would have a pasta dinner (the weekly special) at Howard Johnson's.

We planned better the following year and had a New Year's Dance in the School Hall. I was with Father Zega that evening as he celebrated Mass. He had a heart problem and the doctor warned him about getting a cold at all costs. That night he felt ill and I encouraged him to stay at home and take care of himself. I was pleased when he made his decision to do just that. However, in the middle of the night Father Garvie took him to Hackensack Hospital because he was so sick. He died that morning of viral pneumonia and our parish mourned the loss of such a good friend and great priest. Chet's father had a gold watch and when his son became a priest, he had it converted into a pyx, which was used to bring Holy Communion to the sick. The family gave this pyx to me and I will always cherish it as one of the greatest gifts I ever received.

Because Chet had a congenital heart problem, the doctor requested that they perform an autopsy. The doctor felt the results could benefit family members with the same problem. They asked me to convey this to his parents. They were old school and initially devastated with this thought, but to their credit, approved the doctor's request and it is my understanding that a heart valve was diagnosed as the problem and a close relative was helped.

Our parish mourned the loss of a wonderful man and dedicated priest. The Holy Name Society was instrumental in having a memorial plaque and bench built in his memory.

It was during that year that Father Coyle, the pastor, retired. He was not well and would continue to reside in the rectory. Father Garvie was put in charge on a temporary basis until a new pastor was installed. He had no idea what the status of the parish was financially and asked me to help. I was astonished to find the poor boxes in the church overflowing with donations; however Father Coyle refused to give us the combination for the poor box locks. I went over to the church and said a prayer. We desperately needed the money to pay bills. After finishing my prayer, I asked myself what combination he might have used. For beginners, I tried the last four numbers of the church's telephone number. Presto! I piled up all the money in a large basket, went over to the rectory, sat at the dining room table, across from Father Coyle and counted the money. He was as mute as a lamb before the shears. Father Coyle got extremely ill later that year and Maureen went over every day to feed him. She was a better Christian than I.

With the arrival of our new pastor, Father Stanley Adamczyk, the great people of the parish got together with a newly formed parish council and planned a tremendous fundraiser to put us closer to being in the black. There never was an event that required as many man and woman hours as this bazaar. It went on for the entire weekend and the final result was that we lost two hundred dollars. The contractor explained that too many prizes were won. I've always felt we were scammed.

The bills in the parish were overwhelming. For example, we owed Coca-Cola almost a thousand dollars. On top of it all, the Archdiocese was putting together computerized records for each parish, which was sorely needed, but their timing was difficult to contend with. A friend of Father Garvie, an accountant, offered to help. Finally, we knew how badly broke we were.

In an attempt to help solve our problem, I ran an Art Show. My brother always helped me with such ventures and this was no exception. Starting off we realized that we needed at least two qualified judges for this event.

My brother planned travel arrangements for a woman named Penelope. He was her counselor of choice at the Auto Club. She was held in esteem at the Metropolitan Museum of Art in New York City and she agreed to volunteer her time and be a judge. We also asked an art teacher from our high school. Her name was Pauline. The Art Show was a social and financial success. Young children paid a dollar and entered their artwork. They used water paints and crayons. Students showed a promising future in the art world and hobbyists showed wonderful talent. It was about this time that Penelope was a no show. Later, it was determined that she fell on a Fifth Avenue bus and broke her leg. Pauline was also a no show and the eager artists were demanding that their paintings would be judged immediately as they had other commitments. Some of them were yearning for recognition for their masterpiece. Maureen and I put our heads together. She said that there were nuns across the street at Mount Saint Andrew's Villa and everyone knows that nuns teach art somewhere, sometime. So across the street I went while Maureen and my brother stroked the art mob. As I entered the Villa, a ninety five year old receptionist informed me that all the nuns, except one of them were away on retreat. I asked where the one nun was and was told, "Somewhere back there." Needless to say, I felt awkward going into the unfamiliar rooms of a nun's residence but there I went in desperation. As I entered the many rooms, I would call out, "Sister Mary." However, I had no success. Finally, I entered a room where a young woman was fixing a door. She was dressed in jeans. I inquired, "Sister Mary?" and she spun around holding a screwdriver as a weapon, asking, "Who wants to know?" I explained the reason why I was there but she acted as if she'd recognize a scam anywhere. I told her I was the Deacon from across the street at Annunciation but she doubted me. I explained how desperate I was and she finally agreed to judge the paintings but she explained that she only studied art as a minor. She got into her nun duds and accompanied me to the school hall. At that moment, the other judge, Pauline walked in. I introduced them and they proceeded to determine the contest winners. An eleven-year-old girl won best in the show. Her father also won a prize. I didn't think a girl that young was that talented but I hoped that I was wrong.

Maureen and I also held a garage sale. The idea again came from the Social Concerns Committee of the Parish Council. In a discussion with one of the parishioners, Tex, he could provide us with a trailer and we could deposit donations in it until the big day came. This was ideal because we couldn't clutter the school and church grounds. A couple days before the sale, we moved everything into the school hall and an army of women marked each item. Flea market dealers and collectors were drawn to the event like a magnet. They came early and offered to buy certain items. They would pile them up in front of us and make an offer. We told them they'd have to wait until the sale started. However, we decided to take their items of choice and put them on an auction block.

We were inundated with clothes and most of them were rags. Also, at the last minute, we received donations of furniture. Already, we were thinking "what will we do if no one buys this stuff?"

So many people participated in the sale. The volunteers spent countless hours putting the items on display and pricing them. Teenagers joined in and added spirit. My brother took over the auction. It was amazing how he raised a tin container that once held tea. He asked for a dollar and several hands were raised. Then he went for two, then five. Surprisingly, it sold for one hundred and twenty dollars. Phil and Paul were present and expressed interest in buying a Polaroid Camera that seemed to be in decent shape. They offered twenty-five dollars but we told them it was going to be auctioned. They didn't understand the concept despite several explanations. When the bidding started on the camera, Frank asked for an opening bid of a dollar; Paul shouted out, "I'll give you twenty-five." We called them aside and said we'd take five dollars if they would leave and they did, like thieves in the night. We set up one of the classrooms with clothes. The shoppers appeared to be people in need. Maureen set up shopping bags. Some of them were very large and some very small. We put up a sign, "a bag full of clothes for one dollar." Almost every piece of clothing disappeared in the large bags. Several purchasers felt guilty and asked if there was a mistake. We told them, "No, use a large bag or a small one;" it made no difference. Maureen's idea was a good one. We helped the poor with this gimmick. Everything was going well. The day brought in plenty of money and the parishioners came together. There was one ripple. We didn't sell much of the furniture and we had no place for it. The sale was almost over. At that time, a young couple entered the hall and started looking at the couch. The asking price was twenty-five dollars. They were definitely poor so Maureen and I told them we'd give it to them for five dollars. You could see the contentment on their faces. We then told them that the two end tables and the coffee table with the lamps were lumped together. Tears of happiness came down the young woman's cheek. They told us they had an apartment with no furniture. Another problem arose. They had no truck. We told them that delivery was included and we got some volunteers to accompany them home. This final sale was the crème de la crème. We all went home that night knowing that we had a tremendous day.

Unfortunately, Tex disappeared and we had his trailer in our lot for almost six months. Finally, we tracked him down and officially closed out this fundraiser.

Working at the Auto Club in those days had perks for the travel agents. Huge discounts were offered on airfares for families. Maureen wasn't interested. She went to Ireland the year before we were married and one of the plane's engines went on fire at the airport in Ireland. We did take advantage of the discounts offered on Cruise Lines. Our first venture was on the Franconia of the Cunard Line. We only had to pay the taxes and our trip to Bermuda will always be remembered. Denis was seven and Brian was three years old. We sailed during the first week after Labor Day and had the time of our lives. Denis and Bea Moloney, my in-laws, sailed with us on a Greek Line Cruise to Nassau in the Bahamas. We were a tightly knit family.

It was sad when Bea Moloney had a massive stroke in 1976. She was sent to Burke's Rehabilitation Center in Mamaroneck, New York where she made slight progress. While she was there, Maureen used to go across the George Washington Bridge every night and pick up her father. They would visit Bea and head for home. One evening after Maureen crossed the bridge, the hydrogen tanker in front of her crashed into an overpass and went on fire. Maureen and a young man got the driver out of the van. Despite her small stature, she carried him to a ditch and dove for cover as the overpass was completely blown away. After the incident and after the police, fire department and ambulance arrived; she was directed into a detour and got lost. She got home late with blood all over her leather topcoat.

The next morning we received four telephone calls from the truck driver's daughters. Each one thanked her for saving their father's life. He was recuperating in the hospital. He lost an eye but his condition was no longer considered critical.

That year we were invited to the Annual Fort Lee PBA Party, which commemorated civilian heroes. Maureen and the young man who assisted in the terrible accident were honored. The access from the bridge in that area was closed for months while the overpass was replaced.

When Bea was sent home from the hospital, it proved extremely difficult for Denis to get her out of their apartment. The trip to and from the elevator and getting down four or five steps with the wheelchair was awkward and rather dangerous. We put our heads together. They couldn't move to Long Island without a car. It was too remote. The obvious thing to do would be to move in with us but Denis insisted that they have their own privacy. We'd have to add on to the house. We mutually agreed that this arrangement would be the best for everyone. It was necessary for me to take out a home equity loan, which I couldn't afford. However, Denis agreed to pay for the addition and I agreed to let them live rent and utility free for the rest of their lives. Denis was getting crotchety at the time. He had a tremendous burden taking care of his wife. Naturally, Maureen would help him when the move was finalized. I outlined what had to be done to the house and Denis objected time after time. Adjustments to the plans were made and we went through all the legal requirements and were ready to start building. Denis then changed his mind and wanted to switch the bathroom and kitchen locations. To keep the peace, I complied with his request. The addition was built for a handicapped person and I did most of the work, learning as I went along, until it was finished. Denis and Bea came out to see the final product and Denis said, "I've changed my mind." Bad luck to him! Maureen and I were now stuck with an addition that we couldn't afford. She was very upset that her father did this but I assured her that things would work out.

Two years later, I was in the hospital with ulcers. I wonder why? My dad was at Mount Saint Andrew's Villa when he suffered a massive stroke. When he was released from the hospital, he came to live with us. This had to be the most challenging time in my life. Fortunately, we had space in our addition, on the main floor with no steps. I used to get up early in the morning, wash him up, make the bed, square away the room and get ready for work. I hired a senior friend and neighbor to keep him company during the day. He would make him tea and toast and entertain visitors from the Villa with tea or wine. The main complexity was getting the always-dangerous "Snoopy" to accept my dad's helper. After several days, they became the best of friends. It is so discouraging taking care of a loved one under such circumstances. Initially, Doctor Rigalosi, who I felt, saved my father's life, said he wouldn't be able to come to the house because his practice was so busy. It would be necessary to get a doctor who makes house calls. I inquired if there were anyone like that in the world. He recommended a Dr. Gabe Sinisi who just finished his residency at Holy Name Hospital and had no office as of yet. Well, Gabe took good care of my dad and we found him an office in Paramus and became his patients and friends.

One day, I went down to my father's room to clean him up for a new day. It was not uncommon for him to ring the buzzer on his bed all night and this was one of his worst mornings. I walked into his room and he looked straight at me with glassy eyes and said, "Who the hell are you?" His mind wandered at times but never like this. I was tired and said, "I'm Harry!" Then I proceeded to the bathroom to get some clean clothes and water. When I returned, he inquired, "Where's Harry?" I told him that Harry was lazy and useless and I fired him. A puzzled face was washed away as I got him cleaned up. It was about a month later when he asked me, "Have you heard from Harry." I told him, "Yes." He was doing well and got a job with the New York City Transit Authority. My dad responded, "He'll have to work now." My dad had no use for the Transit Authority. He worked for them for forty-four years. It seems that in monthly intervals, he'd ask again about Harry. Each time I would tell him that Harry got another promotion. At this juncture, Harry was on their Board of Directors and became a despicable character because he could have only gotten into upper management if he was well connected and knew somebody.

At the time, a gentleman photographer and writer from, The Advocate, the Archdiocesan Newspaper came to our house. His name was Dan. He was doing a story on run away teenagers and we were helping out in this area in a big way. Therefore, he came to interview us. Maureen and I had a cup of coffee with him when my father awoke from a nap. He asked what the noise was and we told him that it was my dad who had a serious stroke. He was sorry to hear about it and was quite amazed that we handled things so well for the children and took care of my dad as well. He asked if dad liked company. I told him that he loved visitors. He said he'd say hello. We then proceeded to my father's room. As we walked in, he spotted Dan, clenched his fist and said, "Harry, you son of a bitch, where the hell have you been?" Maureen and I broke out laughing and were unable to explain to Dan what it was all about. Finally, when the laughter stopped, we explained. Then it was his turn to laugh.

It was on October 16, 1976 that I walked into dad's room and he, knowing well that the Catholic Church was going through the formalities of selecting a new Pope, said to me, "Son, we're going to have a Polish Pope!" I thought he had really flipped his wig. However, that day the announcement was aired that Pope John Paul II was chosen and he was from Poland.

He became seriously ill that evening and passed away at Holy Name Hospital in Teaneck, New Jersey.

14

A TRYING ACT OF MERCY

One day I was sent by my pastor to help a young man named Ronny who was depressed. As I understood it, he was handicapped and his wife had left with his very young daughter. Normally, this was not the kind of case I worked on. However, I went to see what I could do. When I arrived at his house, I rang the bell. A voice cried out, "It's open." When I entered the house, I noticed that almost all the furniture was gone; he informed me that his wife took it when she left. He was in a wheelchair and only had the use of his right arm. Both of his legs and his left arm were disabled. It took a while, but I finally got around to asking him about his disability. He said he couldn't remember with certainty but he had been a New York City Police Officer living in Rockland County. He was getting ready for work and thinks he reached for his firearm and it went off and stuck him right between the eyes. He married after his rehabilitation and he and his wife had a daughter. Unfortunately, they had irresolvable marital problems and she had recently walked out on him. I asked specifically what I could do for him. He said that he needed someone to get him up in the morning and put him to bed at night. He had a neighbor, Mrs. Green, who offered to do his shopping for him. He took care of the house himself unless it was something demanding in the way of a major repair or reaching for something. He had gimmicks to help him get things out of his reach, like a can of food. He said he had other problems but getting him up in the morning and putting him to bed at night were his immediate needs. I told him that I would take care of this personally and I would eventually get volunteers to lighten the burden. He was thankful, and with his instructions, I put him in his bed for my first time. He had a duck (a plastic bottle) if he had to pee during the night.

The next morning, I arrived at his house early because I had to go to work. He actually complained because he wasn't used to getting up at 6:00 a.m. I thought initially that he was kidding but I realized he wasn't. I told him that I had a life too; if it's too early get someone else. The desperation mode kicked in and he became a gentleman immediately. I could have taken the time to explain to him that I had a job and the responsibility of a family but he had to realize this, so why bother?

After getting him up, I went back home, kissed my wife good-bye and walked to the bus stop where my commute began each day to 33rd Street and 7th Avenue at the Penta Hotel in New York City.

During the day, I was distracted on my job. I kept thinking how I might alleviate the situation with Ronny. That evening when I went to tuck him in, I realized that we had things to discuss. First, I told him I wasn't his peon and wouldn't allow him to crap on me. He apologized for the foul language he used on me in the morning and he truly appreciated what I was doing for him. I then told him that he could learn to get into his bed at night. He said that wasn't possible. He insisted that the bed was too high. I suggested that I cut the legs in half. This way he could roll into the bed from his chair. Naturally, he didn't like the idea but I told him that I frequently worked late in adverse winter weather and again in the travel season. He said he'd mull it over. I told him I'd give him time; he had two days before I stopped coming at night. He said he sometimes watched television when he was in bed but has to stick with the same channel and if the horizontal or vertical goes on him he's tormented through the night. These were days when there was no cable or remotes. I rigged up a broom handle for him with a modified hook to turn the TV on or off. Then I wrapped a piece of Velcro at the end of the stick to solve his fine-tuning problems. He liked my spontaneous inventions and elected to have me cut the legs. Before he changed his mind, I got a saw which I had in the car. After all was said and done, I told him it was time for a trial run. He took the dive and landed in an awkward position but was able to straighten out his body. The stick proved to be a real success but it was important that it was within reach. What was really a priority was the need for a phone at his bedside. He never needed one up to now but if there ever were a fire, he'd be screwed. I notified the fire department that the resident at 198 Thomas Drive was handicapped, and they put something outside his door to alert firefighters should an emergency arise.

Since Ron was an ex-cop he quickly won favor with the men in blue. However, he crossed that imaginary line several times when he indicated he needed assistance and all he wanted was a six-pack.

At the next Holy Name meeting, several guys volunteered to get him up in the morning. Several of them were retired and made life easy for Ron, getting him up at a reasonable time. It became a job for me on Saturday mornings only. It freed me up to do other things.

When I explained to the Holy Name Society that I was concerned that he had no phone access in the event of an emergency, my friend, Charley Musumeci, said he'd take care of it. He ran UNICO, an organization comprised of men of Italian descent. They bought him a cordless phone, which was the latest craze, and they installed it on the wall next to his bed. This organization responded several times to make life more bearable for Ron.

One of my closest friends was a police officer named Al Smith. Al became the Sunday morning volunteer. The two of us used to love playing gags on Ron but we were very concerned about his welfare and we were quick in solving any unexpected problems that arose. He had a brother who lived in Rockland County and another who was a State Trooper in upstate New York. Although he said they were close, I rarely saw them at Ron's house.

Ron had now begun to work his way back into society. Prior to his wife leaving him, he was cooped up. Now, he was making friends with volunteers who were helping him and they welcomed him into their lives.

My neighbors Dot and John Lewis invited him to every New Year's Eve Party they had. Before taking Ron to the annual blast, I warned him that I had to work on New Year's Day and I would have to leave the party at 1:00 a.m. If he decided to stay he'd have to figure out how to get home on his own. At 1:00 a.m. he was singing away and as I anticipated wanted to stay later. John and another friend, Ben Ireland, said they'd take him home. I tried to explain that they had to follow a few simple rules in transporting him but they had enough beer to be experts on this matter. So I took off across the street to my house and went to bed.

I was told that Ronny wanted to go home about six in the morning. Ben and John put him in the car. It snowed heavily that night and everything was extremely slippery. They pulled up on Ronny's driveway and got the wheelchair out of the car, putting it next to the front passenger seat. Ronnie managed to stand up and his legs locked in place because of the braces he wore. At that point, John and Ben slipped on ice and the two of them with the wheelchair slid down the incline into the pile of snow the plows left behind them. Ron was holding on to the window frame of the front door but his hand slipped uncontrollably and he started down the driveway unaided. John and Ben almost sobered up instantly when they observed what had happened but broke into laughter when Ron cried out, "A miracle, I'm walking."

Our parish agreed to supplement Ron's pension by having him run a parish hotline, a job that was created for him. He used to answer questions relating to entitlements and he operated an assurance line. He used to call elderly parishioners who were living alone to make sure they were okay. This went over so well that our neighboring parish, Our Lady of Visitation got in on the act. They provided a similar service using Ron for their hotline. He did a great job for all of us. He also called the members of different parish organizations to remind them of meetings. This increased interest in the parish while at the same time helping Ron. It was a perfect job for him because it demanded intelligence. Many of the jobs offered to people who are physically challenged are insulting. Corporations give them menial low-paying jobs such as selling light bulbs or putting creases in cardboard packaging that machines don't do well. One time, he accepted a position from an insurance company to monitor a radio they supplied. They wanted to know about every fire in Newark. There were so many fires and Ron thought he was going to make a real killing. At the end of the month, he was told that the city wasn't Newark, New Jersey but Newark, Delaware. He called them and said, "Get this damn radio out of my house."

There was a young college graduate who just landed a job at Easter Seals. She told him that her specialty was occupational therapy. She discussed many possible jobs that he could work at home. The one that was the most appealing was raising plants. He became quite knowledgeable about perennials and annuals. He also got a donation of pots from many of my friends and he loved giving a plant to someone who helped him in a special way. The young lady was pleased about her decision for recommending such work and sat down to talk to Ron. She told him it was time for him to give up his social security and go into the plant business. He said to her that she was brain dead if she thought for one minute that he would give up what was keeping him alive. She then got pissed and actually threw a plant at Ron. He retaliated immediately and threw one at her and this went on for about half an hour. The end result was that she was fired and mounds of earth were all over his normally kept spic and span domicile. The next day was Saturday. Yep, it was my turn to get Ron up. As I walked in, the door was unlocked as usual; I asked what happened before I got to his bedroom. He yelled, "Don't ever give a penny to Easter Seals." I gave him the usual buttered roll and cup of coffee and cleaned up the mess. After that day, I always sent him Christmas cards cluttered with Easter Seals.

One day as I was leaving his house, he asked me to mail some letters for him. I told him I would but asked why he was putting stamps on bills. I asked him why he didn't have the utility pay the postage due. At first he didn't believe this was possible but I convinced him that it was. From that day, he never put postage on bills until the post office announced that they would not deliver mail without postage. He was fed up and said he was disgusted. The Post Office General really screwed up a good thing. When he told me this, I sent him a letter with phony letterheads pointing out that he was the worst violator in Paramus and they would be especially vigilant of every piece of mail that comes out of his house. He fell for it hook, line, and sinker. He didn't believe me that I sent the letter as I had anticipated, so I told him to flip the letter and see my initials on the back. He cursed me out but calmed himself down when I told him that I figured out a way to beat the system. He asked me for the answer but I told him I would have to test the system to see if it works. I went home that day and mailed a letter which read, "The system works." Then I wrote the envelope as if Ronny wrote it and I put my name as the person the letter was being sent to. I then mailed the letter without postage. Timing is everything. I was there when he got the letter. He looked at the envelope and said "That's strange I never remember mailing this." The envelope was stamped. "Return to sender, postage due." He was puzzled, opened it and read the note. He laughed.

He enjoyed going each day to Bergen Pines Hospital as a volunteer. He did clerical work and they treated him to lunch in their cafeteria and frequently gave him food to take home for dinner. This was like another paycheck for him. He enjoyed the company, the challenge of the job and the income. One beautiful sunny day, his ride to the hospital didn't show up. He was so upset that he decided to push his wheelchair from his house to the hospital. This was about a half-mile hilly trip. Nevertheless, he started his trek. It was just about at that time that a mentally insane criminal escaped from the mental hospital in a wheelchair. Unbeknown to Ron, he continued on his bold venture of independence. A new patrolman on his tour of duty for the first time without a fellow officer heard the call on his police radio and spotted Ron. He pulled up, adjacent to him, and traveling at the same slow rate of speed said, "Pull over!" Ron retorted in a manner of obvious annoyance, "Was I breaking the speed limit?" Then he said, "Do the police have nothing else to do except harass the handicapped?" The officer was very iffy about this stop and called for the supervisor who happened to be Lieutenant Al Smith. Al arrived on the scene and told the officer that he and his partner Gunther would take care of it. The officer was tickled pink and left the scene. Al then drove Ron to the hospital where he reported for work. Getting out of the police car he warned Al not to tell Joe Niland. Naturally, Al said he wouldn't say a word. Al called me immediately and the next morning when I walked into his house, I said "Well, I hear you made a perfect ass out of yourself yesterday." He cursed out Al for divulging this unbelievable occurrence.

One time, he asked for advice. He said he'd like to put a very manageable shrub on the lawn in front of his picture window. I said I knew a friend that had a prune bush he was giving away but if he wants it, he'd better let me know as soon as possible because he'd be giving it to someone else. It's a very expensive shrub and can't be out of the ground for an extended period. Ron corrected me and said, "You mean a plum bush," but I insisted that it was a rarity and was a prune bush. When I went home, I called Al Smith, knowing well that he would be interrogated the next day and he was. Ron asked him if he ever heard of a prune bush. Al said yes but he couldn't afford one on a cop's salary. The next time I went to Ron's he said he'd like to have the bush. Ron's brother was going to pick him up that weekend so I told him I'd put it in the ground for him. Al and I planted a dead bush and bought three boxes of prunes and scotch taped them on the dead branches. Needless to say, Ron was elated over his newfound treasure.

My dad was still alive and used to call him to see how he was doing. Both of them were hockey enthusiasts. My dad loved the Philadelphia Flyers and Ron the New York Rangers. Ron didn't know it but many of the games were taped in the afternoon and put on TV in the evening leaving one with the impression that the game on TV was live. When the Rangers and Flyers were playing, my father would get the score and call Ron to bet a six-pack. He would always give Ron a spot knowing well that he would always lose by one goal. Sometimes the goal that made the difference was scored in the last seconds of the game. The next day, my father would call him and tell him to forget the six-pack; he only wanted to teach him a lesson.

We had a lot of fun together but over seventeen years I had to get replacements for people he bad mouthed and abused. One morning I went over to his house to get him out of bed. He cursed and swore at me like never before. I told him to knock it off. He didn't, so I put down the newspaper I always bought with the coffee and buttered roll and I left. He never called nor did I.

I felt I performed my charitable work for Ron. Many friends of mine helped him after I left. They were all abused in some way but were better Christians than I and turned the other cheek. It was not a matter of my harboring ill feelings toward him; he had a tough existence. By now you'd probably expect that I would have said, "Bad luck to him," but I felt sorry for him. All the time I dealt with him, I did my best to hide my feelings.

It's not unusual for someone who is physically challenged to be abusive towards others. I'm not a psychologist and possibly they're angry with the rest of the world because their lives are hampered with an affliction that is not shared by others. It is always heartwarming when someone who is physically challenged is so nice to others despite their handicap. I always prayed for Ron. He recently died and his epitaph in my mind is that he died a lonely man. May he rest in peace?

15

A DEACON AT WORK

When I became a Deacon, I thought fellow clergy members would greet me with open arms. This was not the case. Humility was a lesson to be learned. It would have been nice if my ministry was at least well received by the pastors at Annunciation Church but I never felt it was. That is until Father Mike Sheehan took the reins. He recognized the fact that I was not a theological pro but accepted me for who I was. He is a wonderful priest. He took over the responsibility of Annunciation when there was a lack of life, a need for reconstruction and a wanting for money. These were problems that existed since my family arrived in 1968. He has solved the problem of lifelessness, financed rebuilding and raised the financial awareness of the people. He has energized and converted the people who were at one time spectators in our church into Ministers of all sorts. He identifies their assets and inducts them into the army of Christ. He is a fantastic homilist and is also respected beyond the walls of the Church. Sadly, Father Mike has served his time and now must venture off on a new assignment; every hand I shake invokes the response, "Isn't it a shame about Father Mike?" The men and women of the parish are heartbroken.

Father Joe Kwiakowski is the other priest assigned to Annunciation and has become a close personal friend. He is one of the hardest working and well-prepared priests I have ever met. His vocation came relatively late in his life and he is an inspiration to anyone pondering the possibility of a priestly vocation. He has not only learned the names of the people of the parish but also their hearts. He has been the moderator of our "JustFaith" program and has brought eighteen parish members together in the love of Christ. This has been the most successful parish activity that I have ever been involved with. It's a thirty-week program and none of us are willing to let it end. Father Joe is a remarkable guy.

Father Joe replaced Father Bill who left the priesthood. Bad enough he didn't hold true to his priesthood commitment, but he spoke of his dissatisfaction to several parishioners before he left. He questioned the tradition of celibacy and spoke of his poor health and caring for his parents. Within a short time after leaving, he got married in a Protestant church. Many people, who knew him as a parish priest, confided in him and went to confession to him wonder if his commitment to hold their secret thoughts will be kept quiet or does this too have a statute of limitations.

We also had Monsignor Raymond Pollard, a semi-retired weekend Associate Priest for thirteen years. Although he was elderly, he was always up to snuff. You would sometimes see him at the 8:00 a.m. Mass on Sunday and he'd be ready to discuss the impending news that he read in the <u>New York Times</u> and <u>The Record</u> (an anti-Paramus newspaper) that very morning and then deliver a homily with grace. Everyone loved him and they are happy for him that he retired but saddened that his smile, handshake, knowledge and sense of humor are absent from our gathering space. The departure of such greatness leaves a void that can't be filled.

Just recently, I met the new Associate Priest who will help saying weekend Masses. His name is Father Larry Evans. On the first day I met him, I introduced myself as one of the two Deacons of the parish. He said "Your Excellency it's a pleasure." My smile greeted his humorous spirit. I told him he had big shoes to fill. He humbly said, "I'll never be able to fill Monsignor Ray's shoes but I was hoping to make a small footprint of my own. Father Larry is a Chaplain at Paramus Catholic High School and a teacher. He has won over parishioners with his wonderful homilies and warm welcomes. God bless him!

Over the years, I have gotten along well with many of the Assistant Pastors.

Father Chris Bierne was in my opinion a good priest but was under the thumb of the pastor, Father Stanley Adamczyk, who gave his housekeeper more authority than many priests. Father Chris had a good sense of humor and I enjoyed working with him.

There was a married couple in the parish that I considered wonderful friends. They not only cared for their children but the youth of the parish as well. They devoted much of their time serving fellow parishioners. Their son had gone to the Woodstock Music Festival and overdosed on drugs. After that, he became incorrigible and walked the streets of Paramus. He was harmless but unkempt. He couldn't live at home because it would not be safe for his younger brother and sisters. During a cold spell the temperatures plummeted and it was about five degrees. I pleaded with Father Chris to let this young man sleep in the church basement. At first he was reluctant but finally, he agreed. That was on a Saturday night. The next morning I arrived to be Deacon at the eight o'clock Mass with Father Chris. He said, "Good morning Deacon Niland," in lieu of his usual greeting, "Hi Joe." I suspected something was up. I asked him what was the reason for his unusual greeting. He said that we had a miracle take place at Annunciation this morning. I asked what this might be. He said, "We had wine turn into water."

Father Chris Bierne was very kind to my wife who worked at the rectory at one time. The pastor made his life miserable with his two ferocious Doberman pinscher dogs and his Rottweiler housekeeper. Chris won over my respect, not only for his priestly commitment but also for his stamina and endurance in his ministry.

The young man I referred to was a character. Maureen and I tried so hard trying to reason with him but his mind was destroyed with the drugs of yesteryear. His visits to our home resulted in a meal and/or a piece of clothing to keep him warm or comfortable. One time I took him to a ranch for wayward men in Newfoundland, New Jersey. As I left, I felt confident that he turned the corner but as I arrived back in Paramus, he was already walking the streets.

Since my family was so involved with the Fire and Police Departments, we had a radio with their frequencies to insure the well being of our children. One day, a call was overheard that an intruder broke into the rectory. I jumped in my car and was there in about thirty seconds. Our pastor at the time, Father Phillip was in the panic mode as this same young man got a turkey out of the freezer and decided to cook dinner for himself.

Father Phillip ran the parish through a non-functional Parish Council. They were reminded several times that he had veto power over them. Once, Maureen and I organized a group of twelve talented teenagers who wanted to serve others in the community. Before I gave my okay to help them accomplish their dreams; I had them practice. They were intent on doing well. They learned the lyrics to church and popular music, played instruments and wrote essays which were creative and interesting. I asked our Parish Council to listen to them perform and perhaps provide them with words of encouragement. They didn't have the time, so as 'Ole Blue Eyes would sing "I Did It My Way." Bad luck to all of them!

We only went to places where no one else would go. We went to the Geriatrics Section of Bergen Pines Hospital. Many of the patients had no visitors. Some were asleep in wheelchairs and others were sickly and confined to bed. However, those angelic voices from a group I called "The Beatattitudes" put smiles on faces wrinkled with age.

It was challenging when we went to the men's jail. The inmates didn't seem to be hardened criminals and welcomed the kids with applause and when the show was over, they called for an encore. The Sheriff at the time was responsive to the words of Matthew, "Whenever you did this for the least of my brothers, you did it for me."

We then decided to perform at the women's jail. We figured they'd be a pushover but that was not the case. Half way through the performance, the inmates got rowdy. They were cursing and punching each other. The troublemakers were removed and the performance continued. I thought the kids' courage was to be admired and complimented them on their stick-to-itiveness. However, they weren't pleased with themselves and felt it was their fault. They searched for an answer in the critique that followed each performance and decided that they must learn a Spanish song and so they did. We visited nursing homes and made many trips during Christmas and New Year's. They showed greater leadership than the Parish Council.

During Father Phillip's reign as pastor, we had a weekend Assistant Priest who taught at Seton Hall. He was out of my league. Father Frank was a brilliant scholar. It bothered me when he talked over my head intentionally. It was like my mom and dad speaking Gaelic so my brothers and I couldn't get the drift of their conversation. Once, Father Frank wrote a book on Far East Cultures and Religions. I had no interest in the subject but since I assisted him at weekly Masses, I thought it appropriate to read the book and I asked him for the title of the book. He asked me in a chastising voice, "And why would you be interested in my book." I told him that I see him frequently and thought I had the obligation to bear witness to his literary accomplishment. On second thought, I wasn't that polite. He held out his book and gave it to me to read. Well, I read it and it was boring but surely an educational tool for someone studying the subject for college credits. I returned the book to him and thanked him. Now his test began. "Did you enjoy it?" I answered, "Yes." I told him that it reminded me of another book I read. Filled with doubt, he inquired "And what was the name of that book?" I gave him the name of the book and told him that a personal friend of mine wrote it. His name is Philip Yampolsky. Philip was my brother's father-in-law. He was a linguist for the Navy during World War II and was now a professor of Japanese at Columbia University. Father Frank said he would love to meet him and I responded many people would. Father Frank was an educated maggot, bad luck to him!

There was a great priest assigned to our parish by the name of Charles Waiters. He was killed in Vietnam while saving fellow soldiers on the battlefield. The Catholic War Veterans and members of the Knights of Columbus, the Father Charles Waiters Council, honor his memory every year in November. He was a hero and I regret not meeting him. He was assigned to our parish when I was still living in the Bronx.

Father John McCrone was a guy any one could relate to. He was the State Police Chaplain and had the gruesome job of meeting with the families of World Trade Center victims. I assisted him several times at services and Masses. I respect this man for what he accomplished. He can bring you the smile of Christ on his face in a down to earth manner.

Vinny Brock was a Paramus Police Officer who died en route to a bogus 911 Call. His cruiser crashed and he died at the scene. His unfortunate death has been forgotten by many of our townspeople, but Father John meets with Vinny's friends on the anniversary of his death every year. They say a prayer and recall moments of his life that they shared and then they become all too human and down a few brews.

I met Father Dowd from Saint Luke's Parish in North Bergen when he was the Essex County Police Chaplain. He brought two kids to me. One was a runaway teenage boy from Lima, Ohio. He was with us a day when he walked through the glass of our family room door. It seems Maureen had given it a special cleaning as she frequently did. The young man thought the door was open. He was apologetic. It was an accident, and I had no money to fix it and payday was a couple days away. I asked Father Phillip if there was any insurance coverage the parish had of which I could avail myself. He said coldly, "There is no such thing." So I took cardboard and put it in the frame of the door until I could have the glass replaced. Many people think Deacons get paid. My sons tease me by reminding me that no good deed goes unpunished.

Father Dowd also brought a young Columbian teenage boy to my home. My buddy, Al Smith, got involved and I was told that Jorge came home from school and found the house he was living in completely vacant. His mother and father were gone. No one had any idea where they were. It was my understanding that they owned a coffee plantation in Columbia. It sounded like some kind of drug connection but the bottom line was that Jorge Garcia had no place to live. Maureen and I decided to take in George, as we called him. We enrolled him in the high school as George Niland. He lived with us for several years. He was indeed a lover boy. His culture dictated that he should always be polite to the woman of the house and always obey to the letter, the man of the house. All I had to do was whisper and he would follow my directions. It took a while but finally Maureen became a parent in control. George was lazy and didn't want to work. He finally lined up a job but claimed that he needed a car to get to work. Maureen and I gave him a loan to buy the car but he lost his job and used it to socialize with the girls. He got stuck in snow one time and burned out the transmission. The car was now dormant in the driveway. He owed money on it and had no job. Nevertheless, he wanted his freedom. I sense that he made a Columbian connection and disappeared. I forged his name and sold the car retrieving the money he owed me.

Father Dowd was a compassionate priest and was accused unjustly of something. The bishops dishonored him and his case was referred to the Vatican. It took years but he was vindicated. Unfortunately, where does he go to get his reputation back?

Father Garvie was my closest friend. It was devastating for me when he died. He was the one who babysat for my kids when Maureen and I were stuck; he worked hand in hand with Maureen and me in our crisis home for children. We never kept formal records because we never wanted them to be scrutinized and never wanted the State of New Jersey to have a grip in our family. From time to time, the press covered some of the events in our lives. Some of the children came overnight and stayed for over twenty years. Others came for a visit and kept coming back with such frequency that they adopted our family. Maureen and I loved all of them and I'll attempt to tell you some of their stories. Many of our children were foster children. Once DYFS thought they'd honor us by naming us Foster Parents of the Year. It certainly wouldn't make a child feel as though they belonged if we hung that plaque on the wall. Naturally, we didn't accept their alleged honor and couldn't understand their incompetence for offering us such praise.

Earlier I mentioned Paul who came to us from the Edna B. Conklin Home. He was so self sufficient for a young boy! The first night he stayed with us, we made a big fuss. We wanted him to have a sense of security. He went right off to sleep that Friday night and when we awoke that next morning, he was nowhere to be found. I checked under every bed, in every closet and in every nook and cranny of the house. Finally, Maureen and I decided to call the police. As I reached for the phone, it rang. It was my neighbor, John Lewis. He asked if we took in another child. We told him we did and he's missing. John said he woke up and there was a strange kid between him and Dot in their bed. He asked her, "Dot, who the hell is the kid?" They figured out the puzzle within a short time.

Lillian was a sweet girl who had a tendency to get depressed. She was angry with her mother and father because they refused her the possibility of having a social life with her high school friends. They were concerned that she'd do something to herself and when Lillian asked if she could stay with us on weekends, they agreed. She always had to check in and was on a strict curfew. Her grades improved and she was delighted with the arrangements. For years, my oldest son, Denis, and Lillian went out to eat on their common birthday. Eventually, we had the honor of witnessing her marriage in Holy Matrimony.

One of Lillian's friend's was Pia. She ran away from home and in her travels found a black lab that was also homeless. I guess misery loves company. Pia had no shelter so Al Smith took her to our house. Naturally, the parents were notified that she was safe and we needed time to work things out. She was sent to share a room with our foster daughter, Mary Ann. She took a shower and then dried off the dog and herself with the new towels Maureen displayed with pride in our master bathroom. As my dear Friend Jim Dade reminds me, "People are important, not things."

Laurie was a wonderful young lady. She came to our house initially as a friend of one of our kids and then as a visitor who frequented our home several times a week. She was very outspoken and shared the most private of thoughts with Maureen. Her father sexually abused her and her sister. It took years but her sister, Rita, snapped and stabbed the father several times and killed him in an airport down South. Rita was not as outspoken as Laurie and certainly not as resilient. She ended up being institutionalized. Hearsay claims she was put in a padded cell for the rest of her life. Hopefully, this is not true, but the mental scars must have been overbearing for her. She was bitter and also came to our house but never shared her inner feelings other than telling us a couple of times that life was a "bitch!" Both sisters claimed that the mother was aware of the abuse but did nothing about it. Laurie's dream was to own a cabin in the Smokey Mountains and to drive a Semi for the other six months of the year. In time she achieved that dream.

One of my recollections was Laurie's visit around the Christmas Holidays. Although she was Jewish, Maureen always bought her a small present. One day, a young man named Gerry, who was also a regular visitor stopped in as Maureen was telling Laura to check under the Christmas tree to see if there was a gift for her. She found her necklace and was tickled pink. Gerry and she were sitting with me at the dining room table. He asked her what her last name was. She told him that it was "Grossman." He said that makes you a Jew. She retorted, "What of it?" His response was, "You're one of those who crucified Christ." I stopped him in his tracks and told him that Laurie was my friend and should never be treated this way. I'll tell you more about Gerry but let me finish telling you more about Laurie. She called our house when she was about eighteen. I answered the phone and she said she wanted to get out of the hellhole she was living in and she wanted me to marry her and her boyfriend, I tried to reason with her, but this was her "out" and she wanted it now. It was necessary for me to explain to her that she was Jewish and her boyfriend was Protestant and I only preside at marriages after couples attend a marriage encounter program and the rite is performed in a Catholic Church. She then asked whom I knew that could do this. I told her if it was a civil ceremony, I could ask the mayor. She said she'd wait for his answer. Well, the mayor couldn't do it but referred me to the mayor of Glen Rock. He married them in the park but not before they arrived on a motorcycle. She was clad in her wedding gown, which flowed in a stream from the wind generated by the bike's speed. She put the wedding on hold until her bridal party arrived in the back of an ice cream truck. They embraced and kissed and embarked on a life together that was short lived and ended in divorce. However, Laurie has a child that she loves and brings fulfillment to her life.

And now, back to Gerry. He used to bring us real high-brow religious music. I think one of the albums consisted of a thousand nuns singing Latin praises to God; certainly not my style of music. I'd rather Joni James and Nat King Cole. He meant well, but told me that his uncle was in jail and if anyone got in my way, his uncle could arrange something. This poor young man needed psychiatric help. We encouraged him to pray and seek help. He knew we were his friends and we were trying to help him. We couldn't do anymore, as he needed professional help.

Once, we had a runaway who was mixed up terribly as far as his faith was concerned. Despite a caring mother and father, he would do outrageous things such as dress up in an alb and walk the streets. Once, he came to our house garbed in an alb and Maureen, Father Garvie and I took him home to his parents. They arranged for psychiatric help for him.

Al Smith and his sidekicks, Detectives Gunther Klink and Richie DeAngelo, brought many kids to our house; each with their own story. One night they brought two young girls that they picked up for hitchhiking. Both of them were fourteen years old. One was the daughter of a police officer. She had been incorrigible for a couple years and this seemed to be the straw that broke the camel's back. Her father filed a formal complaint against her and she was admitted into the Juvenile Detention Unit in Paramus. The other girl seemed to be a decent kid who was carrying a heavy burden but wouldn't discuss it with anyone. This was Maureen's forte. It took five minutes and she spilled the beans. She was attending a public school in Rockland County and was raped by a young man who attended the same school. She wanted to have no charges brought against the young man but feared every day of confronting him. Her "A" average went to "C" in no time and her life was absolutely miserable. She said her mom and dad were Italian-American and devoted to her. They wouldn't understand her dilemma. I asked her if her attitude would change if she went to another school. She said "Yes" but knew her parents didn't have the money to send her to a private school. We called her parents to tell them that their daughter was safe and invited them to our home. With tears in their eyes, Maureen and I related to them what had transpired. The girl's grandfather accompanied them and said he would spend his last dollar on this child that he adored and said he'd pay the tuition. To make a long story short, there was much crying and kissing and finally they all left arm in arm. It seemed strange to me that a change in school would solve her problem, but then again, there's the power of prayer.

We called once a week for several weeks and determined everything was going well. With all the assurances we received, we left it in the hands of loving parents and grandfather. Her grades went back to "A" and she made new friends who reinforced her well-being.

About three years later, I was invited to a Youth Mass at the Don Bosco Shrine in Haverstraw, New York. It was a wonderful sunny day and the young people invigorated the celebration in a special way. At the kiss of peace, a young lady ran into my arms and said, "Mr. Niland, you and your wonderful wife saved my life." I had no idea who she was but looking over her shoulder, I spotted her mom and dad. She had grown into a beautiful young woman. The smiles on her parent's faces told the whole story. She was about to go off to college and had been awarded a scholarship at a renowned university. That night my prayers were of thanksgiving.

I have witnessed many miracles in my life. My neighbor Frieda told me that her daughter and her husband wanted a child but so far, they were left disappointed. Doctors would not give her any encouraging hopes and told her that she would never be able to conceive. I told her that I knew if I prayed to Our Blessed Mother, our prayers would be answered. I told Frieda "I was sure and told her to call me on Valentine's Day with the good news." She called me two days after this feast day with the good news. Thomasine now has three children. One of them is adopted.

Once, during the Advent Season, I was standing near the crèche, which the Holy Name Society sets up each year. This crèche is where Donna Muscarella's dad has donated several animals including the, "Holy Cow." Yes, he was a Yankees fan. While I was shaking hands, a young man asked me where he could buy a shirt. I told him that we had blue laws and he couldn't buy a shirt in Paramus despite the fact that it was the largest retail center in the United States. He expressed immediate disappointment because he and his wife flew in from Michigan for a wedding and he forgot his shirt. I told him not to worry. I explained that I had a large family and had his shirt size in his color of choice. When we arrived at my house, half of the family was enjoying breakfast. I explained to Maureen what the situation was and she looked at the young man and said you're a fifteen collar and a thirty-four sleeve. He agreed and she asked what color he'd like. Pink was the rage at the time and so she offered him two different shades. We then invited him for breakfast but he declined but said he'd enjoy a glass of milk. Then he said that he would have the shirt cleaned and would mail it back to us upon his arrival at his home. Maureen then said, "Are you a doctor?" He said, "Yes." He inquired how she knew. She told him by his hands. There were no calluses, which was an indication that he didn't do manual labor. With that, he laughed and said he'd mail back the shirt. We told him not to bother but to help a child without insurance someday. He said he'd do both.

It was only about a week later when a parishioner's child ran away from home. She was burdened with a pregnancy and her parents were so upset; they threw her out of their house. After she was gone, they felt remorse and confided in us. They had no idea where she could be. We encouraged them to tell the police and pray. Maureen received a call from that young lady and she was a mile from the doctor's office in Michigan.

She returned home on a bus and her parents greeted her with open arms. They are now proud grandparents and their daughter has a couple more kids.

Teenagers are frequently hard to figure out but each one has a formula. Sometimes it takes a lifetime to figure out what it is, and sometimes the problem can be solved so easily.

There was a young lady who had seven brothers and sisters. Her grades were poor and she expressed no interest in schoolwork. Her parents were broken hearted. Their other seven kids were no problem but they couldn't understand their daughter. She too ran away and Al Smith brought her to our house. Her problem was unique. She said she was only happy when she was around horses. She was a beautiful young lady but had no interest in the opposite sex. She'd rather sweep manure in the stables. Maureen asked her what her real problem was. At first, she said "You won't believe me." We assured her that we would and she said she needed a private spot to call her own. She loved her parents and knew they couldn't afford adding onto their house but she needed a place that was private and only hers. She didn't care how big it was as long as it was secluded from the hustle and bustle that filled her home each day. I asked if there was anywhere in her house that she thought would be appropriate to solve her problem. She said that there was a closet big enough for a desk and a lamp. She could get a drape to close it in and that would be fine. In disbelief, we encouraged her parents to try to accommodate her. They did and the problem was solved. She excelled in school from then on, rode and cleaned up after horses on the weekend and eventually found the man of her life after she completed college.

We also had the opportunity to help younger children but the youngest was an infant. I was going off to work one morning and there was a basket with a baby in it outside my front door. At first, I thought we got a gift basket but after a brief investigation, I determined that it was a baby. I called out to Maureen before leaving and told her of my discovery. She thought I was kidding but that genuine cry convinced her that I was telling the truth. I went off to work and left the puzzle and the baby for her. She called the police and Al Smith started making calls. He determined that the "Evergreen Motel" had a young pregnant lady as a resident. It was also determined that she had given birth. Father Garvie and Maureen went there and they found that the young lady was desperate. She had no means of support and her parents would not help. Well, Father Garvie spoke to the parents and they folded like a cheap camera and agreed to take her and the baby back home. They went to my house to see their granddaughter and they were in awe, then they welcomed their daughter and new relative into their humble abode. They helped to raise her but the birth father never had an interest in his child, 'bad luck to him!

Maureen and I were members of the Police Chief's Association of Bergen County." I never attended a meeting. They were held during the day while I was at work, but we maintained a crisis home and we frequently received special referrals from the police. It has been our experience that the police are available twenty-four hours a day to help kids. Cops have been a greater influence on young lives than all the "shrinks" in the world. Sometimes, a child needs a break at a critical time in its life. If a cop is only interested in aggressive behavior with a young person, "bad luck to him".

I have found, however, that a police officer can be the catalyst that helps a young person realize that he or she has a choice to make and let it be a good one. Perhaps, this connection influenced two of my sons to become police officers.

One day a representative from The Division of Youth and Family Services stopped by en route to another destination. She brought with her a young man who had been burned by his parents. He was only nine or ten years old and the burned flesh distorted part of his neck and face. While he was waiting for Maureen and the caseworker to finish their conversation, he drew an ink painting that was so professional that an adult who was art-fully inclined couldn't do better. I treated him to ice cream while they were chatting and he gave me the painting. I still have it buried away somewhere in this house of memories.

One of the most difficult encounters we came up against was with a kid named Scott. It was called to our attention that there was a home for young men in Duchess County called "The Green Chimney Home." This twelve- year old had no place to go for two weeks when the place closed down for staff vacations. All of the other children went home with their parents for this short period of time. They delivered Scott to our house and without any special instructions left us to cope with the unbelievable.

He was in the house for about an hour when we heard screams at our above ground pool. Scott was trying to drown my youngest son in a temper tantrum. Naturally, I ran to his rescue. I yelled at Scott and told him he should never do such a serious thing again. He went into the house and retreated to a closet where he sat in darkness. I figured he'd respond to the call for dinner but I had to talk gently to him and ask him to eat. He finally relented and had dinner.

The next morning, I went to work. Maureen decided to visit a girl-friend's house for a coffee klatch. While the women were enjoying their sojourn from reality, Scott went down in the basement and pried the locked desk open. Wouldn't you know it, there was a German Lugar and ammuni-tion in the adjacent drawer. He came up from the basement and held the women at bay. Maureen was a smooth talker and got him to give her the gun.

Needless to say, it was time for a phone call to report the incident. It was then determined that Scott was on a heavy dose of medicine, "because of his problem." They neglected to mention this to us. After he was given the medicine, we were a little relaxed in his presence. They offered to take him to a temporary shelter but we said we'd handle him and we did. He was a different child once he was medicated. We were told that he had a twin brother. His parents kept his brother and he was rejected. Then his parents got divorced. His mother remarried and the stepfather also rejected Scott. It was no wonder that the kid was mixed up. During his stay with us, I took him to Temple. I felt as though I was an alien in the Temple and, unfortunately, he did as well. He was never encouraged to practice his Jewish faith. I encouraged him to speak to a Rabbi and someday he could receive his Bar Mitzvah.

The two weeks were up and Maureen and I decided to take all the kids for a drive to the Green Chimney Home. When we pulled up, the caretaker ran over and grabbed Scott by the neck. I reacted immediately and flipped his ass to the ground. I asked him what the hell he thought he was doing. He then told me that Scott had beaten their pet donkey with a bat and killed him before he left for our house.

It was a quite trip home. I told the rest of the kids of his sad existence and encouraged them all to pray that Scott will find love someday as all of them had. We all agreed that Scott lived a life of rejection and his parents were his problem. Bad luck to them!

Several years later, there was a manhunt looking for the "Son of Sam." A witness helped draw a sketch of the murderer. When I saw the drawing, it resembled Scott and I dreaded the thought that it could be him. Certainly, I felt he was capable of such a vile act. Thank God it wasn't him!

I could speak volumes about the children that graced our home, but I'd be remiss if I didn't mention Camille. She was about fourteen and was special in so many ways. She was smart, beautiful, and a true warrior. She stood her ground at all times. There was the night that my doorbell rang and our next-door neighbor was holding her son by the hand. She pointed to his shiner and said, "Look what your daughter, Camille, did to my son." I called for Camille and she appeared quickly saying, "I did it and if he pinches my ass again, I'll blacken his other eye." With that, my neighbor retorted, "You did what?" and she whacked her son in the head and departed with an apology. Maureen and I commended her for her action but encouraged her to seek out a more peaceful means of solving problems in the future.

One day, Maureen was at a neighbor's house when I arrived home from work. Maureen always had dinner ready as I walked in the door. I never asked her to do this but it was part of her regimen. This day, Camille was sitting down awaiting my arrival. She told me that she prepared dinner. Actually, Maureen did but she warmed it up. I asked her where the flowers on the table came from. She said they were wild flowers that she picked on the way home from school. With that, the phone rang and Mrs. From, a neighbor, was screaming and threatening Camille. She said a neighbor spotted her picking her flowers. Camille insisted that they were growing wild.

She was the type of kid that could show up at a playground with a hundred children. Within a short period of time there would be fifty against fifty in a melee.

Camille was merely seeking out love and wanted to be a permanent fixture in our house because it was the only place she ever found someone to care about her. She was a live wire. I can't help but recall giving religious instructions to a class one Sunday afternoon. There were eight kids in the class and four lived in my house. I asked a question concerning the homework I assigned. She was the only one to raise her hand. She prefaced her answer by saying "My classmates would have known this if they did their homework." This is how she got the ball rolling.

Maureen and I wanted to keep her as a foster child but her father's situation kept changing and she was tossed back and forth in the system. We lost track of her, but we found out that she was married in Florida years later.

Over the years we helped over three hundred children. Some stayed overnight, some for many years. Some came to chew the breeze and some came with a pressing problem. Some were sent to us guided by the hand of God, some we helped arrange for medical help. We weren't professionally trained to solve their problems, but we did everything we could. Many times, it seemed as though we were the last hope for them. Sometimes we were so inundated with children that there was rarely time to show unique concern for each one of our children, but we loved them all and they all felt that love because we told every one of them that we loved them and reminded them frequently how special they were. The gift of life is the most wonderful thing God has given us. We must cherish it because it can be gone in the blink of an eye. If a person doesn't like children, there is something wrong with them. One of most ludicrous things I ever heard was from a couple who told me they weren't going to have children because of the overcrowding of the earth and the lack of food in the world. I thought about what they said and then I realized that they wouldn't be able to appreciate a child if they had one.

16

AMEN

Thank you for taking this journey with me. This was accomplished because of the urging of my "JustFaith Group." I'm indebted to all of them because Maureen and I have no memory of grandparents or other relatives other than the memories of our moms and dads. We didn't want this to happen to our children's children.

Through it all, we were blessed with wonderful children. My oldest son, Denis, was a Sergeant on the Paramus Police. One day when he was off duty, he decided to organize his garage. He was on his way to Home Depot in Clifton. The one in Paramus was closed because of our wonderful (I mean it) Blue Law. He observed a young woman swerving and skidding. Eventually, she went into the bushes off the side of the road. He stopped his truck, called for help and got out of his vehicle to assure her that assistance was on the way. Furthermore, he told her that he was a police officer and showed her his badge. She was very thankful. He asked if there was anything he could do to help. She said that she felt okay but asked him if she had a flat tire. He started to check when another young woman lost control of her car and squashed him between the two vehicles after colliding with his truck.

He was taken to Saint Joseph's Hospital in Paterson where they initially thought he had a broken neck as well as numerous other broken bones. It was later determined that he had a small bone broken in his knee but he spent months on a blood thinner, to combat numerous blood clots.

Denis was unable to go back to work because of his injuries. He loves photography and is the cameraman for Cops Magazine in New Jersey. He was also elected to the Town Council and loved this job more than anyone knew. He loves getting things done for our town residents. He first became interested in politics when he was a senior in high school. He complained about the inefficiency of The Board of Education. I told him "Don't complain about it to me, you're old enough to do something about it yourself." He ran to secure a seat on the Board but lost by a couple votes to a man who had an impeccable reputation, Mr. Greg Cinnela.

Denis' wife's name is Patty. She always amazes me with her organization and the way she accomplishes chores such as Thanksgiving Dinner with such ease and grace. Not only does all of our family attend this blessed event, but her very large family is there as well. She has wonderful tastes in decorating and always has an interesting gadget that catches my attention and becomes a conversation piece. Patty's personality compliments that of Denis. A family reunion without them would be a misnomer.

Both of them adore children but they never had a child of their own. On August 1, 2008 they handed me a sonogram with what appeared to be a picture of a baby. They smiled. Their beautiful and healthy baby boy was born on March 10 of 2009. This was the answer to many years of praying on my part.

It's a shame that Maureen passed away on January 28, 2002. She suffered for a few years with cancer of the throat and stomach. In my heart, I know she had something to do with this wonderful event. The two of us will share this good news someday in heaven.

My son, Brian, always wants things to be perfect. When he was a little boy, I called him "Lemonhead." He didn't mind this affectionate name, which referred to his blond hair, but he asked me not to call him by this name in front of his friends. He was always concerned about the meaningless as well as important things; and because of this, his friends would tease him. He broke a front tooth while performing on stage when he was in elementary school and the same tooth was damaged or destroyed in various sporting events in which he participated. Once, as a young boy and after another tooth repair job, he came home from school crying. He said the kids in his class were teasing him by calling him "Bluetooth." I took him up to the bathroom mirror and showed him that there was nothing wrong with the coloring of his tooth. He appeared to be convinced and I invited him to help with the grocery shopping. As we entered the supermarket, he looked up at me and lo behold, he had a blue tooth in the middle of his mouth. It seems that the florescent lighting triggered the phenomena. Everything went into the panic mode and we made a trip to "Teeth Incorporated" and remedied the problem.

When Denis and his pals in the Police Department had a party for orphans, they found out that one of them had the Mumps. Although, he was inoculated, Denis came down with this malady but it was a mild version of the disease. After a few days, he was fine. But he gave the Mumps to Brian who had to be hospitalized and ended up getting pancreatitis as a complication. The timing was terrible as he was just about to graduate from Montclair State University and join the police force with his brother. While Brian was in the hospital, his girlfriend at the time brought along with her an acquaintance. Her name was Barbara and eventually she and Brian were married. Denis was the best man at the wedding and as he toasted the bride and the groom, he said, "Were it not for me, this wedding would have never taken place." Everyone was wondering what he was talking about but the bride and groom and everyone close to them had a real belly laugh.

Whenever Brian accomplished a noble achievement that was acknowledged in the local papers, Denis was given the credit.

Brian is a graphic artist and was doing his graphics right up to the time when he had a terrible encounter with fate. He and another cop stopped three thugs from robbing a car at the shopping plaza. The thieves tried dragging his partner and then tried to run down Brian. He ended out banging his head on the windshield and damaging several vertebrae in his neck. As of this date, it is doubtful that he'll be able to return to work.

Brian's wife, Barbara, is a very sweet person. She is an outstanding mother and devotes herself to her family. She is fun to be with and is a person I go to for advice since I no longer have Maureen. For example, after I write a homily, I'll frequently have her read it. She gives me honest criticism but she is never as harsh as Maureen would have been.

She has blessed me with the most wonderful grandchildren. Hayley is the oldest. At this time, she is twelve. She loves people and is always concerned for her valued friends and brothers. She shows signs that she will be an artist someday. She seems to have all of her parent's strong points. It is so unusual for a child to be so intelligent and beautiful.

Gavin is ten and loves sports. He and his father enter a world of their own when he plays in little league games. They can also get lost talking about sports. Gavin lives baseball like most kids his age but his dad loves to play catch with him they way I used to do with him. His favorite sport is baseball and he loves to clobber the ball. His short hair is my good luck charm. Whenever I see him, I give it a rub. He is very creative and loves video games like every other child his age on planet earth.

And then there's Matthew who is five years old. He's my best buddy. We venture everywhere together but I think his favorite spot is the Van Saun Zoo in Paramus. The sheep are his preferred animals. He even has a stuffed toy that he calls "Guy." Don't ask me why. Whenever I'm with him, he makes me laugh.

On his third birthday, I was the Deacon at the Mass celebrated by my friend, Monsignor Ray Pollard. Because he is my grandson, Gavin was serving his first Mass and asked if I would like to introduce him to the congregation. I jumped at this opportunity. All this while my son Denis was taking photographs of this memorable occasion. Normally, this isn't done but it was a situation where fools make rules and wise men break them. The Gospel contained the message spoken by God, "This is my beloved Son, in whom I am well pleased," I introduced Gavin as "my grandson, in whom I am well pleased." We then went back to Brian's house where he had lunch catered. Immediately, I got a great lunch and a nice cold beer. As I sat down to enjoy it, Denis put his laptop in front of me and I proceeded to gloat over the pictures of Gavin serving Mass. Then, Matthew came over and stood by my side and looked at the pictures with me. He said, "Grandpa, that's what I want to do when I grow up." I picked him up on my knee and said "I'm so proud of you; to think you want to serve Mass". He said, "No grandpa, drink beer."

My son, John, has two beautiful daughters, Jamie and Christine. They don't live nearby so we see them infrequently. John is sad about this but says he will always be there for them. This has been proven time and time again. Jamie spent the first year of her life in a cast. She had a birth defect and an operation was necessary to help her walk properly. Her sister graduated from Johnson and Wales where she studied Hotel Management. I pray that we will grow closer and both girls are successful. John's life partner is now Judi.

John was always interested in tools and has learned to master many of them. When he finished high school, he became a firefighter in Hackensack.

He was on the job a mere three months when he was sent to the motor pool to have a truck worked on. While he was there, a fire broke out and killed his entire Platoon. He was the only survivor. I heard the news on television and I rushed to Hackensack, asking everyone with a firefighter's outfit on if they saw John. No one did. I didn't know if they didn't know him or didn't want to give me the bad news. Finally, I saw an arson investigator whom I knew from the Paramus Fire Department. I asked him if he saw John. He said, "He's gone home; he's exhausted."

John loves firefighting and is a Captain in Hackensack and a Captain on the Paramus Volunteer Fire Department. All three boys were volunteers in Paramus and are still members of the Social Department. I serve as their Chaplain.

John bought a home, two houses away from me and down the block from where Brian and his family live. Denis lives on the other side of town.

We are the closest family in town. We make it a point to have breakfast on the third Sunday of the month and we enjoy many dinners together.

Mary Ann is married and lives in Rochelle Park. She has two sons, Ryan and Kevin. Her husband's name is Joe. When Ryan was four, doctors determined that he had a tumor on his brain. It was non-malignant but had to be removed. Otherwise, he would have never seen his fifth birthday. The Pediatric Brain Surgeon from Columbia Presbyterian Hospital spent an extended period of time explaining what they intended on doing. It was not optional. If the surgery wasn't performed, he would only have months to live. The operation took seventeen hours. As he was being wheeled from the operating room, the doctors said he'd probably be non responsive. As he was wheeled past me, I said, "Good man, Ryan!" He looked up and said, "Grandpa!" and then he closed his eyes and went to sleep. The next morning, I was there at 6:00 a.m. Ryan was trying to put on his sneakers. I tried to reason with him, but he wanted to go home. The doctor came in at that time, overheard the conversation and said to take him home. What a great man and great surgeon.

Ryan is an active young man with aspirations of becoming a firefighter. His brother Kevin finished High School and had problems with his hips. He is recovering and plans on attending college at a later time.

Steven is a schoolteacher. He married Ashley, the daughter of a Marine Sergeant from Twenty-nine Pines in California. They have three children

Steven, Jr., Madison and Emma. He calls me frequently. The whole family visited me for two weeks a couple years ago. Steve had a harder time than his brothers and sisters when he came to live with us. He had a tendency to rebel at times which one might consider normal, but he objected to our authority because in his young mind; he felt we were trying to replace his mom whom he held so dear. Today, Steve is a wealth of knowledge and considers himself an authority on children, and why shouldn't he? We have lengthy conversations and share our minor problems with each other. Sometimes our conversations last an hour. Both of us wish we were closer.

Many of the other children usually contact me after Thanksgiving and before Christmas. Maureen's spirit is alive in all of them.

There are many more stories I'd like to share with you but I'll save those for another time. At least my children's children, when they ask about their grandparents, will have this book to remind them of the love we shared in our home with each other and with our children. May God bless them and may God bless you.

EPILOGUE

On December 6, 2010, Brian's wife, Barbara, went to work as a buyer at Toys or Us in Wayne, New Jersey. She showed no signs of sickness during the day. Her friends said she acted as her usual self. But when her workday ended, she walked on a path to the parking lot. She was only a very short distance from her car when she collapsed and took her last breath. A tree was planted at that very spot by her friends to keep her memory alive and to acknowledge the loss of a wonderful wife and mother. My son and his three children were devastated and their lives were drastically changed. Friends waited for hours in inclement weather to say their last goodbyes and hundreds of friends stopped by at their home to offer Brian and the children their condolences.

The saddest moment in my life was listening to Brian tell his children that Barbara, their mother, died. He loved her so much and he cried with his children and told them how important it was to make their mother proud of them.

That spring, my grandson, Gavin, continued playing catch with his dad and his younger brother chimed in. Gavin ended out playing with a little league team that won the New Jersey State Championship. They played many games with his mother's initials on their jerseys. Hayley attends IHA Academy in Washington Township and will be attending college later this year and Matthew attends Stony Lane School. Brian drove for The New York Giants until he was hired by Paramus Catholic High School. He is now the Vice President of Operations and Safety.

My son John has another house. It's located on a lake in upstate New York. He built much of it himself. He is now the Fire Chief of Company 3 in Paramus and continues being a Captain in Hackensack and future Chief of the great town of Paramus, New Jersey.

Denis and Patty love their little cap wearing son Jack Liam. Their five-year old now attends kindergarten full time .They hope to live in New Hampshire in the future. Denis is a free-lance photographer.

Rarely do I see my friend Father Joe Kwiatkowski. He is serving the people of Saint Rose of Lima in Newark, New Jersey. I'm sure that he will continue to inspire them and others that he encounters on life's journey.

And me…….. My health is failing and I'm growing old but I thank God for the wonderful family and friends He gave me.

15930483R00104

Made in the USA
Middletown, DE
29 November 2014